# Hinduism in Europe and America

# Hinduism in Europe and America

Elizabeth A. Reed, A. M.

GYAN

*Published by*

GYAN

Gyan Publishing House
5, Ansari Road
Daryaganj, New Delhi-110002
Phone: 011-47034999, 9811692060
E-mail: books@gyanbooks.com

*Distribution Network*
gyanbooks.com
India, USA, Canada, UK, Australia, France



ISBN: 978-81-212-8606-0 (PB)
First Published, 1914

2nd Impression 2023

*Printed at:* Gyan Press, Delhi.



**Hinduism in Europe and America**
Author:Elizabeth A. Reed

# Hinduism in Europe and America

By

**Elizabeth A. Reed, A.M.**

Author of "Hindu Literature, or the Ancient Books of India," "Persian Literature, Ancient and Modern," "Primitive Buddhism, Its Origin and Teachings," etc.

G. P. Putnam's Sons
New York and London
The Knickerbocker Press
1914

# FOREWORD

HINDUISM long remained on its native soil, but during the last few years, classes have been organised in Great Britain, and on the Continent, as well as in America, for the propagation of misleading representations concerning its doctrines, and the gathering in of foreign coin.

In this expurgated system which is offered at first, many have become interested without investigating the foundation upon which it stands. No doubts need be entertained concerning the real teachings of Hinduism by those who have access to the invaluable series of "The Sacred Books of the East," prepared under the editorial care of Professor F. Max Müller and published under the auspices of England's greatest University. We have here translations of undoubted integrity, but the great cost of the work places it beyond the reach of many libraries, and not only this but the vast amount of literature therein contained presents to the ordinary student a most discouraging prospect.

We can well understand that only an enthusiastic specialist would be willing to devote years of his life to the examination of these thousands of pages of exaggerated statements, and abstruse theories, but common prudence should prevent any one from embracing a fad without making some rational inquiry into its true character.

In order to facilitate such investigation, there is need of smaller volumes giving the results of careful work along these lines—volumes which may be quickly read, and are free from technical terms, so that they may be easily understood. This condensed information is especially needed by young men and women, for they will be obliged to meet in their own land the problems of the Orient. Indeed the time is already here when extensive information and constant vigilance are needed, as recent arrests in our large cities for the immoral teachings and criminal practices of the cult, only partially reveal the extent to which the insidious emissaries of the East have already penetrated our body politic.

When heathen temples are rearing their brazen domes in some of our cities, and these are built with the money of American women, surely it is time to furnish them with some scientific data concerning the real purpose of the system into which they are being so adroitly drawn.

In an earlier and larger work the author has given the historical facts connected with the age and the doctrines of the old manuscripts, together with somewhat copious extracts from their contents; these things will not therefore be repeated here, only very brief expositions being presented with the chronological framework necessary to a connected and accurate outline of the subject.

The object of this little book is to present within the smallest possible compass a correct view of this corrupt cult and also to call attention to the authoritative statements of standard Hindu works upon those points which are most frequently misrepresented and lauded by irresponsible writers and speakers.

E. A. R.

CHICAGO, 1914.

# CONTENTS

## CHAPTER V



## CHAPTER VI



## CHAPTER VII



## CHAPTER VIII



## CHAPTER IX

# Hinduism in Europe and America

# Hinduism in Europe and America

## CHAPTER I

### HINDUISM: A COMPOSITE SYSTEM

Land of Contrasts. Vedaism. Traces of Monotheism. Brahmanism. Caste. Transmigration of Souls.

INDIA is a land of striking contrasts; great salt marshes stretch away for weary miles beyond the fertile valleys where wild bees hang their comb to the rocks and the tiger hides in the jungle. Vast deserts reach across the empire, but there are also luxurious forests where the teak and banyan flourish and the fragrant sandalwood still awaits the coming of the axe men—where much of the undergrowth is covered with vines which burden the air with the fragrance of their blossoms. Arid wastes lie parching beneath the pitiless sun, but not far away the almond and pomegranate spread their flowery banners upon the air and ripen their fruits in the long summer time.

Among her people there is want and woe, side by side with wealth and luxury; the gaunt shadow of famine is thrown across the multitude, while petty kings are resplendent with pearls and diamonds. Low caste victims die of hunger and disease within a stone's throw of the palaces of the rajas who are all unmindful of their sufferings, even a drink of water being often denied them because it would ruin the fountain if any of its contents were polluted by their touch.

The contrasts in their literature are fully as great as in the land and its people. In the songs of the Vedas, and also in the great epics which constitute one grand division in their world of letters, we find poetry of a high order, while much of their later productions is necessarily either ignored by the translators, or given in footnotes of Latin, or even in the original Sanskrit.

The sacred Ganges is fabled to have fallen from the blue fields of heaven, coming down to earth from the divine feet of Vishnu. As the Nile is deified in Egyptian mythology, so also this river is called a goddess. One of her sources is found in a cave of ice and she is praised as Ganga, the daughter of Himavat—Lord of the Mountain of snow; but the river itself is polluted beyond recognition by thousands of devotees. So also the primitive adoration of mountain and storm has been lost in a multitude of opposing theories, and the unclean worship of idols representing gods of evil repute.

Although the term Hinduism may, in a general way, be applied to all the faiths and philosophies of that people, it is more properly used to denote the manifold phases resulting from a combination of the earlier creeds of India. It may be likened to a great banyan tree sending its roots down into any soil and drawing sustenance from all possible sources. It has, however, no unity of design, having borrowed from every available cult and adopted something from all of them.

It has accepted to a certain extent the fetishism of the Negrito aborigines; it has encouraged the adoration of the fish and the boar, of the various deities and their wives, and even stones and trees. It brings oblations to the serpents in the mountain caves as well as to the ocean billows that beat against these rocky foundations.

While no one can become a Hindu who is not thus born, any one can be admitted into the lower ranks of Hinduism. Among the natives all comers are welcome who will bow to the rules of caste, and admit the supremacy of the priests, by bringing offerings to their feet.

Anglo-Saxon admirers are admitted into *the outer circle* upon still simpler conditions—all that is required of them is the adoration of the priesthood, and liberal cash offerings for their support.

*Vedaism.* The primitive faith of the Hindu Aryans is represented in the Rig-veda, which is the earliest form of Hindu literature, and is no exception to the rule that the first literary product of any people, after simple records, is found in the form of verse. The Vedas furnish no chronology —not a single date in all of these productions by which any event, or series of events, may be assigned to a proper place in the world's history. Hence the Hindu imagination runs wild in figures as in everything else, and they gravely assign "millions of years" to the age of any of their books which may be under discussion. Indeed it has been claimed that the songs of the Rig-veda "must have been written before the flood because there is no mention of the flood therein"!

Whereupon Prof. F. Max Müller wittily replied: "If all the books which make no mention of the flood were written before it, what a mass of antediluvian literature we must have!"

The concensus of opinion among the most eminent Orientalists however assigns the composition of the earliest of these hymns to the period between 1500 B.C. and 1000 B.C. There is a reservation however to the effect that later researches may show that they belong to a more modern period.

These sons of the southland watched the heavens for signs of the long-needed rain, and they sang of Indra the storm god driving his tawny steeds across the darkened sky, and using the lightnings for his arrows when he forced the unwilling cloud to give up its treasures.

They felt the terrible power of the tropical sun, and sought to appease his wrath by songs of praise —by bringing oblations to him as soon as he came out of the chambers of the east, with draperies of crimson and purple. They called him by various names; he might be Surya, Aditya, or Mitra, but as his golden chariot rolled across the heavens, they fancied they saw the milk-white horses of the sun.

They witnessed the use and the havoc of fire and sang of Agni, who was represented by the flashing lightnings, and also by the clear flame upon the hearthstone. He was the guardian of the home, the minister of the sacrifice, and was often invoked as the creator of all things.

The all-encircling firmament was called Varuna, who was not only the god of the sky but also the sky itself. He knows the pathway of the birds through the blue ether, and the trackless course of the ships upon the wide ocean, for he is also the Neptune of the Hindus who rides upon the waters, or hides in the caves on the shores of the seas. He fills the halls of night with his presence and draws near to his worshipper with the cooling touch of evening.

The Maruts or Rudras were, like Indra, the gods of wind and storm. They were praised as "shakers of the earth" and besought to tear in pieces whatever fiends might attack the people. They were termed "worshipful and wise" and were supposed to dash through the heavens on chariots drawn by dappled deer.

These Aryan singers called Yama the king of death, he was supposed to be the first of men who died, and he guides the spirits of other men to their destination in heaven or hell. In later mythology he is also represented as the judge of the dead, but not in the Vedas.

The most enchanting of these early deities is Ushas, the fair goddess of the morning, who comes out of the east leading the white horses of the sun. Wearing her garments of silver and tinted pearl, she becomes in Sanskrit poetry "the mother of the mornings" and the infant days begin their journey amidst the clouds that float around her feet.

Thus it will be seen that this early faith was a simple nature worship, and was free from the later pollutions of Hinduism.

It is clear that the Rig-veda gives no support to the offensive ceremonies and customs for which it has been claimed it was the early authority. Although the Vedic writings may contain germs of the later systems, they furnish no support for the theory that after death the souls of men must pass through millions of the bodies of lower animals and even find a place in sticks and stones. There is no hint of wedding children in their cradles, or giving a child of eight or nine years of age to an old man—there is no suggestion of the barbarous practice of burning living women on the dead bodies of their husbands. Neither is there any foundation here for the later usage of human sacrifice. These and other things which are, if possible, worse, are found only in the degradation of the earlier worship.

Beginning with the adoration of the sun and stars, the creeds of the Hindus sank lower and lower until we come to the Puranas of the Middle Ages, when licentiousness becomes a feature of public worship, and even the conduct of Krishna is eulogised.

Far better than modern idolatry was the primitive worship of mountain and sky—of starry heights and ocean billows. Better than the serpent and demon worship of to-day were the libations poured out to the storm king as he swept through the heavens on the wings of the wind. Better than human sacrifice on the altars of bloodthirsty Kali were the hymns to the fair goddess of the morning as she comes through the gates of pearl as "the leader of the days" and marshals her host in golden splendour before the children of men.

*Traces of Monotheism.* In all of the old mythologies, the farther we venture back into the past, the fewer the gods become, until we approach that sublime monotheism which was first revealed to the children of men, and India is no exception to the rule. One of the early hymns contains the following beautiful sentiment concerning the mystery of creation:

Then there was neither day nor night, nor light, nor darkness,
Only the Existent One breathed calmly, self contained,
Naught else but He was there,—naught else, above, beyond.[1]

[1] Sir Monier Monier-Williams's trans. of Mandala, x., 129.

In order to briefly state the leading dogma of an early faith we cannot do better than to give its own formula in three words as stated by its own philosophers: "*Ekam eva adwitiyam*"—"There is but one Being without a second." Nothing really exists but one universal Spirit called Brahman. And whatever appears to exist separately from that Spirit is mere illusion.

This, according to the orthodox Hindu, is the only true Veda. This is the uncompromising creed of true Brahmanism. This, at least according to the belief of the generality of educated Hindus, is the only true knowledge to which the Veda leads.[1] Again in the beautiful hymn to "The Golden Child," we find the same sentiment as in many other places.

The God to whom we shall offer sacrifice,
He through whom the sky is bright and the earth firm,
He through whom the heaven was stablished—
Nay, the highest heaven—
He who measured out the light in the air;
Who is the God to whom we shall offer sacrifice?[2]

Only a few of the hymns, however, seem to contain the simple thought of One Divine Self-Existent Being, and even in these, the idea of one God

[1] Williams, *Hinduism*, p. ii.
[2] Max Müller's prose trans. Rig-veda, x., 121.

prevalent in all nature is somewhat uncertain and undefined. The celebrated "Purusha-sukta," one of the most modern hymns of the Rig-veda, serves to illustrate the gradual sliding of monotheism into pantheism:

> The embodied spirit has a thousand heads,
> A thousand eyes, a thousand feet, around
> On every side enveloping the earth.
> Yet filling space no larger than a span.
>
> He is, Himself, this very universe;
> He is, whatever is, has been, and shall be;
> He is the lord of immortality.[1]

But while the gods of the Veda were few in number, and the oblations to them were comparatively simple, they were continually multiplied during the passing years, until millions of deities now command the adoration, and the money, of the hapless Hindu.

In the valley of the Euphrates we find the same conditions. In relation to the early monotheism of Assyria, it is claimed that Hea was one of the names of the God of Abraham, for Hea is another form of El, and the followers of Hea were evidently monotheistic.[2]

[1] Williams's trans. of Mandala, x., 90.

[2] Rassam, *Trans. Vic. Inst.*, vol. xiii., pp. 190–214. See also vol. xxv., p. 120.

This early form of worship, however, was soon corrupted, and ere long the Assyrians counted three hundred spirits of heaven and six hundred of earth.

In Egypt we find similar historical records. Many eminent Egyptologists claim that the earliest monuments show the primitive religion of the Nile Valley to have been monotheism. It appears that when the Egyptians moved into the country, a thousand years before Menes, they had only one god who was Nu. Surely, this name is closely akin to Anu who is described upon the tablets as the supreme God of ancient Accad.

Maspero and some others take exception to the monotheistic theory but all agree that few deities are mentioned in the beginning of monumental history, and that they steadily increase until they become almost numberless. Dr. W. M. Flinders Petrie says: "Wherever we can trace polytheism back to its earliest stages, we find that it results from combinations of monotheism."[1]

That the people of Egypt were once worshippers of the true God is evident from the prophecy of Isaiah: "And the Lord shall smite Egypt and heal it, and they shall *return*, even to the Lord and he

[1] Petrie, *Rel. of An. Egypt*, p. 4.

shall heal them."[1] The Hebrew word which is here rendered "return" is translated by the same word, or its equivalents, eight hundred and fifteen times in the Old Testament, so there is no room for philological discussion on this point.

Prof. F. Max Müller says: "Polytheism must everywhere have been *preceded* by a more or less conscious monotheism. In no language does the plural come before the singular." The eminent Orientalist shows, however, how easy it was for the early peoples to multiply their deities by having various names for the One God. "As long as these names were remembered as mere attributes of one and the same Divine Power, there was as yet no polytheism, though no doubt every new name threatened to obscure more and more the primitive intuition of God."[2]

Among the early families of China the same great principle prevailed. Dr. James Legge, late professor of Chinese language and literature in Oxford University, was the most accomplished Chinese scholar in Europe, and he went back to a period five thousand years ago, before the time when their earliest books were written, and found the old character which meant God to the primitive peoples of China. He says: "Ti was to the

[1] Isa. xix., 32. [2] *Chips*, vol. i., 348–354.

Chinese fathers, I believe, exactly what God was to our fathers, whenever they took the Great Name upon their lips."[1]

Dr. Legge also gives us the primitive Chinese word for heaven as found in their earliest archives. One of the words also found among these ancient characters represents what we call prayer, or the communion of man with God.

The old inscriptions of South Arabia tell the same story. Dr. Fritz Hommel, a leading professor in the University of Munich, has analysed the names of the early families of this country, and has accumulated a vast amount of evidence to show that the *primitive* peoples of South Arabia were not only believers in the One God, but that they also believed that He was gracious and merciful to those who came to Him in sincerity and truth—that He forgave sinners and rewarded the righteous. Speaking of the polytheism of South Arabia, Hommel says:

> This would seem to indicate that there must have been a time in the history of Arabia when these gods . . . a number of whom were certainly imported from the outside—did not receive worship, and when some higher form of devotion of a type which reminds one

[1] Dr. Legge, *Religions of China*, p. ii.

of what we are told about Melchizedek in the Old Testament must have prevailed.[1]

Brahman in Sanskrit, originally meant Power, the same as El. It resisted for a long time the mythological contagion, but at last it yielded like all the other names of God. . . . This primitive intuition of God, and the ineradicable feeling of dependence on God could only have been the result of a primitive revelation in the truest sense of that word.[2]

*Brahmanism.* Whatever remnants of primeval monotheism may have been found during the Vedic period were transformed under the reign of the Brahmans into pantheism—the doctrine that "He is, Himself, this very universe." The Brahmanic period is placed from 800 to 500 B.C. And during all this time it maintained a strong hold over the people, although it was itself undergoing considerable changes.

The one point, however, which was never yielded was the absolute necessity of sustaining with liberal offerings an exacting priesthood. These men introduced complicated rites which could be performed only by themselves, and for which they must be richly rewarded, hence the people were loaded down with ceremonies on every possible

[1] Hommel, *An. Heb. Tradition*, p. 80.

[2] Max Müller, *Chips*, vol. i., pp. 354-355.

occasion, the whole course of a single service often lasting for months and sometimes for years.

The literature of the period is found in the series of Brahmanas, the oldest of which may have been written seven or eight centuries before Christ. This collection of books forms the second division of the Veda, and they are intended as guides in the performance of complicated ceremonials. Julius Eggeling, the faithful translator of a portion of them, says: "For wearisome prolixity of exposition, characterised by dogmatic assertion, and a flimsy symbolism, rather than by serious reasoning, these works are perhaps not equalled anywhere." Many pages are devoted to the washing of the spoons, and to the particular method of laying the sacred grass upon the altar for the numerous periodical oblations, and for sacrifices in general. Still, they represent the history of the period when the priests had succeeded in transforming the primitive worship of the powers of nature into a highly artificial system conducted very largely for their own benefit.

*Caste.* During the Brahmanic period the rules of caste were brought into vigorous operation and indeed Bhattacharya admits that "caste had its origin in Brahmanical legislation."[1] The priests

[1] Bhatt., *Hindu Castes and Sects*, p. 4.

found their first authority for it in one of the latest hymns of the Rig-veda—a hymn which appears to have been inserted in the collection by the Brahmans themselves. This celebrated Purusha hymn contains the following stanza:

From Viraj was Purusha produced,
Whom gods and holy men made their oblation.
With Purusha as victim they performed
A sacrifice. When they divided him,
How did they cut him up? What was his mouth?
What were his arms? And what his thighs and feet?
The Brahman was his mouth, the kingly soldier
Was made his arms, the husbandman his thighs,
The servile Sudra issued from his feet.[1]

Hence the divine order of caste is represented as follows:

First, the Brahman, who is supposed to issue from the mouth of the god. Every priest is a Brahman but every Brahman is not a priest. They are simply a caste divided into clergy and laity. A Brahman, like a poet, "is born and not made," hence a man of foreign birth can no more become a Brahman than he can become a Chinaman. Their sacred books have no welcome for converts, quite the contrary. The sole function of the "converts" on American

[1] Williams's trans.

or European soil is the contribution of money to a cause which constantly demands more. Therefore when a Frenchwoman can make her living in America by pretending to be, not only a Hindu but even a Swami, it is time for her devotees to investigate the subject in some sane way.

The second in the order of caste is "the kingly soldier" who issued from the arms of Brahma. To this all warriors and kings belonged, hence the supremacy of the priests over the rulers was established at an early day. They pose as "advisers" it is true, but their mandates were often accompanied by threats of curses if they were disobeyed.

The third in order was the husbandman who comes from the thighs of the god, and these, as well as the two castes above them, claim to be "twice born."

The Sudra or servile class is only "once born," and they form the lowest rank; but even they are particular about maintaining their proper position. The man who dresses hair will not clean clothes, neither can a table waiter be hired to carry an umbrella.

Besides these grand divisions, as they may be called, there are many sub-castes which are too numerous to specify. These minor divisions have obtained in many ways. They may have originated in mixed marriages; for instance, a Brahman could have four wives, and could marry a woman belonging to any one of the three lower castes and her children would be the beginning of another class of beings.

We have also an almost endless number of what may be called trade-castes, resulting chiefly from associations of men engaged in the same occupation; these are being constantly created and in them the exclusiveness and restrictions in regard to social intercourse and intermarriage are enforced more strictly than even in the original pure castes of early times. Many of these seem to resemble trade unions and have numerous sub-castes under them. For instance in the North-West, the writer caste has twelve subdivisions, and none of them can intermarry except with the highest of the twelve divisions, and similarly the carpenter caste has seven sub-castes none of whom can eat together.

There is even a thief caste and a murder caste. When a death occurs no man should be carried to the burning-ground except by his own caste-fellows. The arbitrary rules have multiplied almost endlessly among the many divisions, still they affect a man chiefly in the four matters of marriage, food, professional occupation, and funeral rites.

The gross tyranny of the Brahmans is admitted even by the native scholars. Lala Baijnath, the ex-Chief Justice of Indore, in his address before the International Congress of Orientalists, made the following assertion:

Next to his slavish adherence to astrology which form such a prominent feature in the Hindu's daily life, is his desire to serve the Brahmans. Everything good must be given to a Brahman—fresh fruit for the first time in season, new corn, milk of a cow which has calved for the first time, and many other things are given to the Brahmans in every Hindu household before any one of the family ventures to touch them.[1]

Jogendra Nath Bhattacharya, President of the College of Pandits and author of *Commentaries on Hindu Law*, says:

The more orthodox Sudras carry their veneration for the priestly class to such an extent, that they will not cross the shadow of a Brahman, and it is not unusual for them to be under a vow not to eat of any food in the morning before drinking of the water in which the toe of a Brahman has been dipped. . . . When a Sudra writes a letter to a Brahman, it must begin by declaring that the writer makes a hundred million obeisances at the lotus feet of the addressee.[2]

All of the higher classes agree in abstaining from animal food, the eating of which, although formerly

[1] Baijnath, *Trans. Ninth International Congress of Orientalists*, vol. i., p. 142. [2] Bhatt., *Hindu Castes and Sects*, pp. 20–21.

permitted on certain occasions, is now regarded as an offence which is almost a crime. Even to sit in the presence of an Anglo-Saxon who is eating beef is not only sinful, but they claim it produces feelings of disgust far greater than those which an Englishman or an American would feel in sitting beside a Chinaman who was enjoying a feast of boiled rats!

And yet, when Dr. John Henry Barrows, late President of Oberlin College, invited Vivekananda to lunch in Chicago a few years ago, the Hindu astonished his host by ordering roast beef!

Every orthodox Hindu is fully persuaded that water if taken from the filthiest stream, provided it is a sacred river, and used for drinking purposes, or applied to his body, will purify his soul. Consequently, he will eagerly drink it, whereas the purest water is supposed to cause external and internal taint, if it should be accepted from a person of lower caste. Not only this but it pollutes the whole of a well belonging to those of higher caste, if one of the lower caste presumes to drink water which has come from this sacred fountain.

*Transmigration of Souls.* This doctrine, which apparently originated in Egypt, took early root in Indian soil, and has long been a cardinal doctrine of both Brahmanism and Hinduism. It is enthusiastically taught in the first Upanishad of the series,[1] is carried through several of them, and afterward more fully developed in the Code of Manu.

The theory provides an easy explanation of all the inequalities of position, fortune, or even talent, as the rich, the noble, or the mentally brilliant are supposed to be enjoying the benefits of merit accumulated in former lives, while the poor and the diseased are suffering the penalties of sins committed in former bodies. It is said that a thievish Brahman was once driven out of a man's orchard and severely beaten, whereupon the victim philosophically remarked to a friend: "It is all right—in a former birth, this man was my donkey, and I was very cruel to him. He has now repaid me for many a blow!" The fact that very few claim to remember any former birth seems to furnish little or no objection to the theory, as it is supposed that memory is lost at each and every death.

The faith of millions of people in India, for nearly two thousand years, has been built largely

[1] The Upanishads are the third grand division of the Vedas, and the earliest of these philosophical works may have been written as early as 600 B.C.

upon the dogma that each being must pass through 8,400,000 lives, which is the natural lot of all souls. These forms through which all must pass are supposed to consist of 2,300,000 quadrupeds, 900,000 aquatic animals, 1,000,000 feathered animals, 1,100,000 creeping animals, 1,700,000 immovable forms such as trees and stones, 1,400-000 human beings, and although there is no gradual rise in position it is only in this last form that final emancipation may be gained.

It is on account of this peculiar faith that every animal and insect is sacred in India, as even a fly or a flea might contain the soul of a priest or of a near relative. It is said that some of the Hindu visitors to the World's Congresses in Chicago, in 1893, became interested in the hospital idea and went home and built a hospital—not for the suffering women and children, but for the feeding and propagation of loathsome insects!

It is noticeable throughout the codes that sins against caste are more severely punished in future births than are offences against morality, but sometimes there is a sort of poetic justice in the penalties. For instance a man who steals grain will be born a mouse; if he has stolen perfumery, he becomes a muskrat; if he has purloined water he will be reborn as a water-fowl; if he has taken honey, in the next birth he will be a gadfly; he who has stolen meat becomes a vulture, one who has robbed his neighbour of oil, will next make his appearance as a cockroach, while one who has stolen linen becomes a frog!

But these punishments are mild when compared to the penalty for sins against caste. For instance if a Brahman neglects his own appointed caste, he will be reborn as a vomit-eating demon, feeding also upon dead bodies and other putrid flesh.

In all the statutes which govern social life, the immense superiority of the priestly class is the great central point of civil as well as ceremonial law.

> A Brahman, whether learned or unlearnĕd, is a mighty divinity, whether consecrated, or unconsecrated.
>
> Let not a king although fallen into the greatest distress provoke Brahmans to anger (by taking revenue from them), for they, if once enraged, could instantly (by pronouncing curses) destroy him with his whole retinue.[1]

The punishment for insulting a Brahman is something terrible:

> With whatever member a low-born man may injure a superior, that very member must be mutilated. . . .

[1] Manu, ix., 13–14, 317.

A once-born man insulting twice-born men with abusive language must have his tongue cut out. Should he mention their name and caste with insulting expressions, a red-hot iron three inches long is thrust into his mouth."[1]

We can hardly imagine it possible for any beings in human form to invent such horrible punishments, to be inflicted even upon the vilest criminal, neither could a law student believe that such enactments had ever been made if they were not a part of the official decrees in the Code of Manu.

This textbook was probably at first a small collection of local enactments which were handed down orally, perhaps, for generations, but additions were constantly made to it, until it became a voluminous portion of their sacred literature, and was then as now the basis of Hindu jurisprudence. It has secured for itself a degree of reverence second only to that accorded to the Veda. About twenty volumes of this enormous work are still in existence and many of its provisions are judicious and beneficial. The Code is, however, a strange combination of civil and religious law. Besides the infliction of terrible penalties at the hands of the civil authorities, the criminal was often assured of

[1] Manu, viii., 276–279.

still more awful punishments in the various forms through which his soul must pass after leaving his body.

Apparently believing that the subject of hell is one in which many people must be interested, the Hindu philosophers have elaborated it extensively. They have provided extensive accommodations for sinners of all classes and degrees in twenty-one hells of various descriptions, each of which is provided with unpronounceable names in addition to their other horrors. The word-pictures of these abodes of torture as given in standard Sanskrit works are appalling beyond description, but there is no crime so fiendish that it does not become innocent, provided only the culprit be a priest who retains his caste, and remembers a sacred text. Hence it is said in Manu: "A Brahman by retaining the Rig-veda in his memory, incurs no guilt, though he should destroy the inhabitants of the three worlds, *and even eat food from the foulest hands!*"[1]

[1] Manu, book ii., 26.

# CHAPTER II

## BUDDHISM: A PROTEST AGAINST BRAHMANISM

Long Series of Buddhas. Birth of Gautama. Great Renunciation. System of Philosophy. Metempsychosis. Jataka Book. Buddha's Hell. Atheism and Later Polytheism. Death of Buddha. Number of Adherents. Expulsion from India.

IT is claimed the Gautama was the last of a long succession of Buddhas who appear at great intervals in the world's history in a series which has neither beginning nor end. This endless chain, according to their official statements, reaches back into the past for so many *kalpas*[1] of ages that the eons of geologic time are lost in comparison. Gautama, himself, enumerates only eighty-one predecessors beginning with Dipankara, but in one of their standard works it is said: "There are many hundreds of thousands of *kotis*[2] of Buddhas,

[1] According to some authorities, a *kalpa* is definitely stated as two billions one hundred and sixty millions of years. While others express its duration as follows: "Let it be supposed that a solid rock sixteen miles high, and the same in length, and breadth, were lightly rubbed, once in a hundred years, with a piece of the finest cloth, and by this slight friction reduced to the size of a mango seed—that would give you no idea of the length of a Buddhist *kalpa*" (Williams, B., p. 120).

[2] A *koti* is explained as being ten millions.

endless like the sands of the Ganges—the incomparable lords!"[1] When we consider that each of these must pass through multitudes of births, we cannot wonder that plenty of time is required.

*The Birth of Gautama.* Gautama, or Gotama, was the name given him by the family. Buddha was not a proper name, but simply an epithet signifying "the perfectly enlightened one," and besides this the founder of the system has seventeen other titles all of which are significant of different qualifications, or positions. Such a mass of myth surrounds his birth and early life, so many dates are assigned to him, that for these and other reasons, some critical scholars are disposed to doubt the fact of his existence as a real being. The native teacher Bhagwanlal R. Badshah not only denies the existence of Gautama, but asserts that Sakyasink, the son of Suddhodana was the great reformer who founded Buddhism. He says of the man whom he claims was the real founder: "He did not want to call himself Buddha, but he wanted to give the name of Buddhism to the new religion he set up. As he delivered the people from

[1] Sukhavati-vyhua, 4, 6. See also Lalita-Vistara, chap. i., p. 6.

the oppression of the Brahmans the people called him an incarnation of God."[1]

The preponderance of evidence, however, strongly indicates that about the beginning of the fifth century B.C. Gautama Buddha was born, about a hundred miles from Benares. He was the son of Suddhodana, who was a landowner of the tribe Sakyas, and although certainly not a king, he may have been a chief of his tribe. His mother's name was Maya-devi and she was the wife of Suddhodana.

*The Great Renunciation.* The story of the four visions which it is claimed led to his abandonment of the ordinary course of life appears to belong to the mythical traditions concerning Buddha. According to the Lalita-Vistara, however, the story, briefly, is about as follows:

One day while walking in the pleasure grounds, he saw a man who was withered and wasted by age. He enquired as to the cause, and was told that this was the final condition of all who were not saved from it by an early death. Then he returned home greatly disturbed in mind.

Going again to the park, he saw a sick man, and learned that disease too was the common lot.

[1] Badshah, *Trans. Ninth Inter. Cong. of. Orientalists*, vol. ii., p. 139.

Again he saw a dead man, and learned that this also was a portion of the heritage of humanity.

Still later he saw a mendicant friar and asked what manner of man this might be, who appeared so strangely? On being told of the great advantages this man was gaining by renouncing the world, he went away in deep thought.

On returning home he reclined on a couch and the women of his household brought their musical instruments and danced and sang until he fell asleep. Then they lay down and went to sleep also. When he awoke they were still asleep, and the Lalita-Vistara gives the following description of the vision upon which he looked:

> He, the Bodhisattva (or future Buddha) cast his eyes upon the ladies; he looked at them with attention; (he found) some of them had their dresses in disorder; some of them had their tresses dishevelled; some of them had their ornaments scattered about; some had their tiaras knocked off; some had their chins resting on their shoulders, some had their mouths distorted; some had their eyes staring; some had saliva flowing down from their mouths; some were groaning; some were laughing; some were talking wildly; some were grinding their teeth; some had their faces discoloured; some had their arms distended; some had their faces distorted; some had their heads uncovered; some had their faces twisted on one side. . . . Beholding this repulsive scene of the ladies lying on the ground,

the Bodhisattva realised in his mind the idea of the cremation ground. Beholding these, that lord of beings, drawing a merciful sigh, thus spoke in distress: "Alas! How can I associate with the beings here assembled? I must retire to asceticism."[1]

He is said to have arrived at supreme knowledge after long meditation and fasting under the Bodhi tree, or "Tree of wisdom," which is familiarly called the Bo-tree. This tree is, therefore, greatly reverenced by all Buddhists, and the one under which he is supposed to have received enlightenment is continually preserved by replanting new trees in the decayed trunk of the old one.

*System of Philosophy.* Four great truths are said to have been revealed to Buddha as the first result of his long period of meditation. These together make what is called the "Law, or Doctrine of the Wheel." They are:

(1) Suffering exists wherever there is life.

(2) Suffering is caused by desire.

(3) Release from suffering depends upon the suppression of desire and the extinction of being (*Nirvana*).

[1] Lalita-Vistara, trans. by Rajendralala Mitra, LL.D., C.I.E., chap. xv., p. 275. A modern English poet has violated the Buddhistic account by painting this revolting scene in very different colours. The Buddha-karita, however, and other standard works give vivid descriptions of the scene which is here so lightly touched.

(4) Nirvana can only be obtained by following the paths pointed out by Buddha. These paths are eight in number, four of them—right vision, right thoughts, right words, right actions—being applicable to all men, the other four being reserved for monks only.

This system was a protest against the pantheism of Brahmanism which makes God everything and everything God, as primitive and genuine Buddhism was not a religion at all, but merely a philosophy, which recognised no God, no prayer, and no priest. It was opposed to all ecclesiastical organisation, being simply a brotherhood of men who had renounced their families, and claimed to renounce all desire for life—men who had pledged themselves to devote their time to the recitation of the law and "the accumulation of merit" for the sake of their own deliverance from the hopeless chain of transmigration which was taught by the Brahmans. The warfare against marriage and family life excited the opposition of the people, and Buddha himself very soon saw that the practical working of his theories must also bring destitution, as the monks were forbidden to work, but must obtain their living by carrying from door to door a bowl in which they received scraps of food. Lay-brothers and lay-sisters were therefore a necessity;

somebody must work for the support of the monks. Married householders were made members of the outer circle, and the formula for their admission into the ranks was very simple, being merely a repetition of the following words:

> I go for refuge to the Buddha.
> I go for refuge to the law.
> I go for refuge to the Order.[1]

It was also understood that they should abstain from five gross offences, but the principal test of their loyalty was their willingness to serve the monks.

Buddhism was a protest against Brahmanism concerning the tyranny of caste, because it taught that all men were equal; all men too must suffer in their own persons, either in this or in future lives, the consequences of their own acts. And as all actions, whether good or bad, lead to repeated future existences, the great end and object of every man must be to attain non-existence (*Nirvana*) by meditation and the suppression of all action.

It was also a protest against Brahmanism in denying the existence of the soul. The second discourse which Buddha ever delivered was at

[1] Maha-vagga, i., 7, 10.

Benares on the Non-Existence of the Soul. The belief in self or soul was accounted so distinctly a heresy that two well-known words in Pali terminology were coined to stigmatise it. And yet, in defiance of these facts, Dharmapala stood up before an audience in Chicago and said: "I will now read to you some Buddhistic *ideas* in Christian language." And then he proceeded to read the parable found in Luke xii., emphasising verse 20: "Thou fool, this night shall *thy soul* be required of thee." This is only one example of their misrepresentations of their own books and creeds on foreign soil.

*Metempsychosis.* As Buddhism officially and emphatically denied the existence of the soul, it could not in any way recognise the transmigration of the soul. Gautama taught, however, a system of metempsychosis wherein the *character* was transferred from one being to another. Although he admitted the existence of no God, he was compelled to recognise an all-ruling power from which there was no escape and he called this power *karma* or *karman*—action. The substance of this teaching is that the result of what a man does is concentrated in a new sentient being—new in its constituent parts or powers, but the same in its essence, its being, or doing—its *karma!* The theory is that as soon as a man, animal, or angel dies, a new being is produced in a more or less painful state of existence, according to the character or actions of the creature that died. Rebirth as an animal clearly forms part of the oldest Buddhistic belief and later works rightly take it for granted. In the Dhamma-pada, which is one of the oldest Buddhistic works and claims to reproduce the sayings of Buddha, he is represented as declaring:

> Through countless births have I wandered, seeking but not discovering the maker of this, my mortal dwelling-place, and still again and again have birth and life, and pain, returned.
>
> But now, at length, thou art discovered, thou builder of this house. No longer shalt thou rear a house for me. Rafters and beams are shattered, and with *the destruction of desire*, deliverance from a repeated life is gained at last.[1]

*The Jataka Book.* The Buddhist scriptures are spoken of as consisting of nine divisions, and of these, this collection forms the seventh. Although it is briefly called the Jataka Book, its full title is, "The Commentary on the Jatakas," as it not only contains the stories of previous births, but also explanations, and a description of the cir-

[1] Dhamma-pada, 153–154.

cumstances under which they were told. The date of this work, like the others, is undecided, but T. W. Rhys Davids, the translator, says: "The rise of our Jataka Book was due to the religious faith of the Indian Buddhists of the third or fourth centuries before Christ," the statements therein contained having been handed down orally from time to time until they were committed to writing.

In several other standard works of the sect, the *karma* of Buddha is represented as having belonged, and apparently in succession, to both men and animals. He is represented as not only remembering many of his early experiences, but also of repeating his adventures in former births for the instruction and entertainment of his followers, and these are the stories, of which he is always the hero, which are gathered in this great collection.

It is said there are five hundred and fifty different births, concerning which tales have come down to us, and in some of the Buddhist temples relics of Gautama are exhibited, such as hair, feathers, and other fragments of animals whose forms he formerly wore.

According to the Jataka and other standard works, he was born once each as a fairy, a hare, a frog, a water fowl, a carpenter, a devil dancer, a silversmith, a gambler, a curer of snake bites, and a dog. Twice he lived as a pig, twice as a thief, twice as a rat, and he also repeatedly led the lives of a jackal, a fish, a woodpecker, and a crow. Forty-three times he was a tree-god, and twenty-four he was a teacher, in twenty-four also he was a courtier, and he led twenty lives as a king's son. In three lives he was an outcast, and in three a potter. Four times each he was born as a peacock, a serpent, and the god Brahma; in four lives also he was a horse, and afterwards lived in four different bulls. In twenty-three lives he was a nobleman, and in twenty-two a learned man. Five times each he was born as an eagle, and as a slave. Six times he was an elephant, and six times a snipe. He lived eight lives as a wild duck, and ten as a lion. In eleven births he was a deer, and in twelve a man of property. Thirteen of his lives were devoted to commerce, and in eighteen forms of existence he was a monkey. "The noteworthy point," says Sir Monier Monier-Williams, "about the repeated births of Buddha, is that there was no Darwinian rise from lower to higher forms, but a mere jumble of metamorphoses."[1]

It is true that he is represented as being born in the Tusita heavens the last time before he was

[1] Williams, B., p. iii.

born as Gautama, but, says Oldenburg, "This in no way implies that a superhuman existence is claimed for him. One who is a god in one existence may, in the next, be born as an animal, or he may be born in hell."[1]

If he be born in hell, he is not thereby debarred from seeking salvation; and if he be born in heaven as a god, he must sometime leave his happy estate, and seek for the condition of the perfect man who has attained Nirvana, and is soon to achieve the only consummation for which it is worth while to live—extinction of personal existence in Pari-nirvana.[2]

Although the Bodisat (or future Buddha) passed many lives in the humble forms of the frog, snipe, rat, serpents, monkeys, and others—although he repeatedly lived as thieves, outcasts, and gamblers, yet he escaped the greatest humiliation to which he could have been subjected in the eyes of the people of India in that he was never born as a woman!

*Buddha's Hell.* The descriptions of hell are very graphic and the doctrine of *karma* contains no forgiveness. "Not in the heavens," says the Dhamma-pada, "not in the midst of the sea . . . wilt thou find a place where thou canst escape the

[1] Oldenburg, B., p. 324. [2] Williams, B., p. 122.

force of thy evil action."[1] A passage in the Deva-duta-sutta represents Yama as pronouncing the doom of a wicked man:

> These, thy evil deeds, are not the work of others, thou alone hast done them all; thou alone must bear the fruit. And then the warders of hell drag him to a place of torment, rivet him to red-hot iron, plunge him into glowing seas of blood, torture him on heaps of burning coals; and he dies not, until the last residue of his guilt has been expiated.[2]

Although the punishment of hell is not eternal, its shortest duration is five hundred of the *years* of hell, each day of which equals fifty years of earth. Buddha's own description of the future punishment of a backbiter is found in the Maha-vagga; a portion of it is as follows:

> To the place where one is struck with iron rods, to the iron stake with sharp edges he goes; then there is for him food as appropriate, resembling a red-hot ball of iron. . . . Then he who commits sin is surely boiled in a mixture of matter and blood; whatever quarter he inhabits, he becomes rotten there from coming in contact with matter and blood. . . . There black-mottled ravens eat them who are weeping, and dogs, jackals, great vultures, falcons, and crows tear them.[3]

[1] Dhamma-pada, 127.

[2] Deva-duta-sutta, trans. by Oldenburg.

[3] Maha-vagga Kokaliya sutta, ii., 19. The Buddha-karita gives, if possible, a more terrible description than this, and it is

*Atheism and Later Polytheism.* "Buddhism has no Creator, no creation, no original germ of all things, no soul of the world, no personal, no impersonal, no supermundane, no antemundane principal."[1]

The idea of a Creator is not only denied, but Buddha claimed to find no being in the whole universe who was his own equal.

An ascetic by the name of Upasaka came to him to enquire of whom he had learned his philosophy, whereupon Buddha replied as follows: "I have no teacher; there is no one who resembles me. In the world of gods I have no equal. I am the most noble being in the world, the irrefutable teacher, the sole, all-pervading Buddha."

But he did acknowledge the various gods of the Hindu pantheon, and it will be remembered that he claimed to have been born as a tree-god forty-three times.

These gods or spirits were very much in the order of precedence and were all (except Mara, the Evil One) supposed to be passably good Buddhists. They were not feared but patronised as a sort of fairies, usually beneficent, though always more or less foolish and

---

there described as a part of the enlightenment which Buddha attained under the Bo-tree, and this was "the true knowledge" which was attained in the second watch. See Buddha-karita, bk. xiv., 10, 6.

[1] Williams, B., p. 117.

ignorant. . . . No exception was made in the case of Brahma. He also was evanescent, was bound by the chain of existence, the result of ignorance, and could only find salvation by walking along the eight-fold path. . . . But even if the idea of Brahma were the same as the idea of a god, union with him would mean merely a temporary life as an angel in the Brahma heavens.[1]

The radical atheism of Buddha resulted in extravagant polytheism among his followers. He taught that man has no Father to whom he can appeal for sympathy and aid, but the higher sentiments of the human heart naturally reach upward, seeking some object of veneration, and no one can set his affections upon a system of philosophy. Hence there are now multitudes of gods in the Buddhist pantheon, and many of them are mentioned even as early as the Dhamma-pada.

The Buddhism of the North became connected with Shaivism, magic, and even with Tantrism or Shaktism with all its loathsome accompaniments. Without apparently making war upon existing faiths, it still claims that a man may be a good Buddhist and at the same time anything else he pleases. Not only this, but it absorbs other creeds or assimilates some of their ideas. For instance in Japan it has embraced Shintoism,

[1] *Sa. Bks. of the East*, vol. xi., pp. 163–4.

while in Ceylon and Burma it has included serpent worship, and the adoration of demons, with all of which, as well as with the recognition of many a Hindu god, it is still connected. Although at first opposed to all organisation except as a roving band of monks, it now has an organisation similar to that of the Roman Church with the Grand Lama reigning as Pope. Idol worship also soon came into vogue and during the reign of this cult in India, the monks vied with each other in the ingenuity with which they constructed their idols. They were made to give out light, or flash glances from their crystal eyes, and were also furnished with machinery that would enable them to nod, or reach out a hand to bless a worshipper who was liberal with his offerings.

It is not strange that atheism should lead to polytheism as the other extreme, and that idols are now more abundant in Buddhist countries than among any other idolatrous people. Even in Chicago, at what is called their "devotion meetings," after a very flowery and very misleading address, incense is burned before the image of Buddha, and men and women go through with the various forms of obeisance before the idol.

*The Death of Buddha.* The official and only reliable story of the death of Gautama is found in the Maha-parinibbanà Suttana, or Book of the Great Decease, which is supposed to have been written by some of his devoted followers at a time when reliable traditions concerning the matter were still in circulation among the people. Very briefly, the story is as follows:

At Pava the Blessed One stayed at the mango grove of Kunda [pronounced Chunda] the coppersmith. Now at the end of the night Kunda made ready in his dwelling place sweet rice and cakes and a quantity of dried boar's flesh.

And the Blessed One robed himself early in the morning, and taking his bowl, went with the brethren to the dwelling place of Kunda. And when he was seated, he addressed the worker in metals, and said: "As to the dried boar's flesh you have made ready, serve me with it, Kunda; and as to the sweet rice and cakes serve the brethren with it."

"Even so, Lord," said Kunda. And the dried boar's flesh he had made ready, he served to the Blessed One, whilst the other food, he served to members of the Order.

Now the Blessed One addressed Kunda and said: "Whatever dried boar's flesh is left over to thee, Kunda, that bury in a hole. I see no one, Kunda, on earth, nor in Mara's heaven, nor in Brahma's heaven, no one among gods and men, by whom, when he had eaten it, that food can be assimilated, save by the Tathagata." "Even so, Lord!" said Kunda. And whatever dried boar's flesh was left over, he buried in a hole.

Now when the Blessed One had eaten the food prepared by Kunda, there fell upon him a dire sickness, and sharp pain came upon him, even unto death. But the Blessed One, mindful and self-possessed, bore it without complaint.

He did not die at once because of his indiscretion, and before he passed away he exonerated Kunda from all blame in the matter:

"This is good to thee, Kunda, and gain to thee, in that when the Tathagata had eaten his last meal from thy provision, then he died. The offering of food, which, when a Tathagata has eaten he attains to supreme and perfect insight, and the offering of food, which, when a Tathagata has eaten, he passes away by *that utter passing away in which nothing whatever remains behind* . . . these two offerings of food are of equal fruit, and equal profit, and of much greater fruit, and much greater profit than any others."[1]

The body of Buddha was cremated, and the remains were divided into eight parts, one of which was assigned to each of the parties claiming it. Over each portion of the relics a mound was built and a feast was held.

It is probable that in this important work, which is one of the series of *The Sacred Books of the East*, we have much of history, not only because it is one of the oldest of the Buddhist productions,

[1] Maha-parinibbana Suttana, chap. iv.

but also because it records events which would not be allowed in a work of fiction. Orientalists have called attention to the great improbability that the followers of Buddha should fabricate a story to the effect that he died from eating too much pork, in view of the fact that he had always forbidden the killing of animals. Many animals were held to be especially sacred because Buddha was supposed to have lived in such forms in previous births, and he was born twice as a pig.

*Nirvana.* This term was not original with Buddha as it was certainly current before his time, and it is still common to both Brahmanism and Buddhism, and the native authorities present so many contradictory expositions of it, that it has become a problem among scholars. The meaning of the word is "extinction," "blown out," or "the state of a blown-out flame." The Buddhist who arrives at eternal rest is supposed to be "blown out like the flame of a candle." But we cannot expect such a term to be explained always in the same way, by a system which is so elastic that it changes front to a greater or less extent, in order to suit the opinions of every people whom it approaches. Buddha himself frequently spoke of his impending death as "the final extinction of the Tathagata." Sir Monier Monier-Williams argues that Nirvana is not in itself necessarily the annihilation of all existence, it is the absence of pain and also of demerit—the absence of all thought and all work. "It is not consciousness, neither is it unconsciousness."[1]

Besides Nirvana, we have another term—Pari-nirvana; that is, "without remains or remnants of the elements of existence."[2] This is the oblivion to which Rhys Davids refers when he says: "Death, utter death, with no new life to follow, is the *result* of Nirvana."[3] It is what Williams calls "The extinction of personal existence in Pari-nirvana."

Hence, although there are various shades of thought and definition, Oriental scholars agree that the *summum bonum* of the Buddhist ambition is the absolute nothing; the only question being whether Nirvana itself is utter extinction, or only a half-conscious condition which is to be succeeded by eternal oblivion. It is true that Buddhists seeking converts in Christian countries claim that: "Nirvana means union and communion with God—the absorption of the soul in the Divine essence"! But no position can be more absurd than this in

[1] Williams, *Buddhism*, p. 141. [2] Childers's Pali Dictionary.
[3] Rhys Davids, *Buddhism.*, p. 114.

view of the fact that genuine Buddhism believes in no God with whom union could be formed, and no soul to be absorbed, if indeed it did recognise a Divine Being. Max Müller says:

> Buddha himself was certainly an atheist; therefore if Nirvana was not, in his mind, complete annihilation, still less could it have been absorption into the Divine essence.[1]
>
> True wisdom (according to Buddha) consists in perceiving the nothingness of all things, and in the desire to become nothing, 'to be blown out,' to enter into Nirvana. Emancipation is obtained by total extinction . . . if to be, is misery, then not to be, must be felicity, and *this is the highest reward that Buddha offered to his disciples!*[2]

*Number of Adherents.* It seems to have become the fashion for some people to announce that "a majority of the human race believe in the doctrines of Buddha," and others, though less thoughtless, are giving currency to the statement that out of the fifteen hundred millions of earth's inhabitants, at least five hundred millions are Buddhists!

It should be remembered, however, that Buddhism has virtually disappeared from India proper, although according to the census of 1901, they claimed more than half the population of Burma and its borders, where the most of them in that

[1] Max Müller, *Chips*, vol. i., p. 284. [2] *Ibid.*, p. 227.

region have congregated.[1] Its strongest position is in China and Japan, but in China, the principal religion is Confucianism. The best authorities upon this subject, including the late Dr. James Legge, Professor of Chinese in Oxford University, are of the opinion that there are not more than one hundred millions of Buddhists in the world.

> I should be surprised, [says Prof. Legge,] if it were proved that there are one hundred millions of men in this world who would write down, or direct another to enter, their names as believers in Sakya-muni (or Buddha) and his doctrines.[2]

Although the question of the truth or falsity of any position can never be indicated by the number of its adherents, still it is well to ascertain the numerical strength of any people so as to be able to estimate, to a certain extent, the influence which they may have in the world of thought.

According to the most reliable information which can be obtained concerning the present status of the principal religions of the world, they rank in point of numbers as follows: Nominal Christianity; Confucianism; Brahmanism and Hinduism; Buddhism; Mohammedanism; and lastly Taoism (the system of Lao-tsze); Jainism;

[1] Encyclopedia Britannica.

[2] *Trans. Ninth International Congress of Orientalists*, vol. ii., p. 580.

Zoroastrianism; the others being too small to be considered in this estimate.[1] Thus it will be seen that Buddhism numerically occupies the fourth place, although its adherents are fond of declaring that their creed "controls the thought of the greater portion of the world's population"! Science however must deal with facts and not in fanciful speculations. The incredible figures claimed by Buddhists must have been obtained by calculating the entire population, in every country where the system has a foothold. Or they may have been obtained as were the figures of the Buddhist priests who returned to India and told the people there, that at the "World's Congresses" which they attended in Chicago in 1893, they "made thirty thousand converts to Buddhism"! When this story was indignantly denied by Dr. John Henry Barrows they promptly qualified it by saying: "Well we made one convert who was worth as much as thirty thousand common men"!

*Expulsion from India.* The expulsion of Buddhism from India, or rather its extinction by absorption and amalgamation, was a gradual work to which no very definite period can be assigned.

Even in Benares, the Chinese writer Hiouen Thasng found it flourishing side by side with

[1] Williams, *Buddhism*, p. 15.

Brahmanism in the 7th century of the Christian era. In other parts of the country there was probably a period of Brahmanical hostility, and in some cases, perhaps, actual persecution, but Buddhism was drawn back by the Brahmans, themselves, who finally pacified the followers of Buddha by boldly claiming that he was one of the incarnations of Vishnu! This doctrine of the avatars was not fully developed until we come down to the Puranas about the middle of the Christian era. The old Brahmans, having discovered the efficacy of compromise, overcame opposition by this means and thus enticed the seceders back into their caste system. Only a small section of the Buddhist community resisted all attempts at amalgamation and the successors of these are the Jains. Jainism appears to be the only sect in India which represents Buddhistic ideas and this is a near relative of Buddhism if not its actual descendant. There is no reliable proof that any religion bearing the name of Jainism existed before the time of Christ. And yet, an advocate of this system, in a public address in Chicago, in 1893, declared: "*My religion was old, when the pyramids were young!*" No wonder that Sir William Jones remarked: "The comprehensive mind of an Indian chronologist has no limits!"

# CHAPTER III

## DEVELOPMENT OF HINDUISM

Combination of Theories. Burning of Widows. The Yoga Philosophy. Brahma. Shiva. Ceremonies. The Tantras. Kali, Wife of Shiva.

HINDUISM is Brahmanism modified by the influence of Buddhism, and it appears to have adopted nearly every doctrine of the later cult except its atheism, its denial of the existence of the soul, and its levelling of caste distinction.

It retained the pantheistic idea of Brahmanism: "There is One Being and no second," but it is supposed that the One Supreme Being amuses himself by illusory appearances—that He is manifested variously, as light manifests itself in the rainbow; and all visible objects, human beings and animals, are all emanations from Him and will eventually be absorbed into His essence.

While Hinduism is often theistic or pantheistic, it is always polytheistic, the various theories being constantly interwoven into each other, and hence more than a hundred millions of the people of

India are bewildered with the strange tenets of a creed which combines the teachings of monotheism with the worship of a multitude of idols—which declares at one time there is but one God, and still constantly inculcates veneration for many of the Hindu deities.

From the few gods of Vedaism, the pantheism and polytheism of the Brahmans, and the atheism of Buddha, the Hindus have evolved a system under the rule of which their pantheon contains three hundred and thirty million objects of worship.

This later cult has succeeded in embracing something from most other available creeds, and in presenting phases suited to many minds. It proclaims belief in the efficacy of sacrifices, rites, austerities, and penances, and these are still called "the way of works." It also advocates faith in multitudes of personal deities, and this is called "the way of faith and devotion."

*Burning of Widows.* This horrible rite has certainly been found in India as early as 300 B.C., and Raja Radhakant Deb, the great Hindu scholar, claims that it was practised from very remote times; it surely flourished there to a very alarming degree during the prosperous reign of Hinduism. At the close of the 18th century seventy widows were burned alive with the body of one of the rajas.

It was not practised by the Buddhists, but with all their reverence for animal and insect life, we have no record of any effort being made by them to even curtail this unparalleled cruelty. They were afraid to kill a snake or other reptile lest it might be a new form worn by some of their ancestors; they were too humane to kill a flea, or more revolting insect; but they looked indifferently on, while women were burned to death from one generation to another.

When British rule obtained, a guarantee was given the natives that they should have liberty of conscience—that their religious rites should not be disturbed. When, therefore, the officers of the government began to protest against these brutalities, the priests stoutly declared that it was a part of their religion—that it was sanctioned by the Veda, and the English could not touch it without breaking their solemn pledge. When they were asked to show European scholars the text in the Veda which sanctioned such barbarism they answered that their "holy manuscripts must not be desecrated by the touch of an unbeliever!"

When, however, they learned that the government was in earnest—when they were reminded that while they were to have liberty of conscience, they would not be allowed to commit murder in its most cruel form, if it could be legally avoided, —then they deigned to produce their "evidence." Raghunandana and other doctors actually quoted chapter and verse which they claimed to be from the Rig-veda, and Colebrooke, one of the best Sanskrit scholars of that period, was obliged to translate it according to their assertions. Dr. Horace Hayman Wilson, however, at last obtained the manuscripts, and discovered that the documents which were too sacred to be profaned by the hand of a foreigner had actually been violated and falsified for the purpose of perpetuating this horrible practice.

Prof. F. Max Müller well said:

> This is perhaps the most flagrant instance of what can be done by an unscrupulous priesthood. Here have thousands and thousands of lives been sacrificed and a fanatical rebellion threatened on the authority of a manuscript which was mangled, mistranslated, and misapplied. . . . The Rig-veda, which now hardly one Brahman out of a hundred is able to read, so far from enforcing the burning of living women, shows clearly that the custom was not sanctioned during the earliest period of Indian history.[1]

When the dishonesty of the priesthood was

[1] F. Max Müller, *Chips*, vol. ii., p. 34.

exposed, Lord William Bentinck suppressed the crime, for the Hindu dignitaries found themselves one morning face to face with a decree which they could not escape nor disannul. It is said, however, that even now, living women are sometimes burned in remote districts, and under conditions of secrecy which prevent discovery by the King's officers. And yet, in defiance of the historical facts, when a self-styled "swami" in America was recently questioned on this subject the answer was: "It is true that some Hindu widows have *preferred* to be burned on the dead bodies of their husbands, rather than to meet with a worse fate at the hands of the English soldiers!"

A more cunning falsehood could hardly be devised, in view of the fact that according to the Hindu authorities, themselves, this horrible rite obtained for more than a thousand years before a British soldier ever set foot on the soil of India!

*The Yôga Philosophy.* There are several systems of philosophy in India, but that which seems to be most strongly advocated among moderns is the Yoga, which was founded by Patanjali.[1] It is a branch of the Sankhya, but in Europe and America it seems to be more popular than its parent.

[1] The time of Patanjali is still a debated question, but Max Müller places him after the third century of the Christian era.

The aim of Yoga is to teach the means by which the human soul may attain complete union with the Universal Soul. This fusion may be effected even in the body by the constant habit of keeping the mind in its unmodified state—a state clear as crystal when uncoloured by contact with other substances. The eight means of mental concentration are as follows: Restraint; religious observances; postures; breathing in a peculiar way, or in the suppression of the breath; restraint of the senses; steadying of the mind; contemplation; and profound meditation, or a state of trance which is most effectually attained by such practices as fixing the eyes intently and incessantly on the tip of the nose.

> The Yoga system appears in fact, [says Williams], to be a mere contrivance for getting rid of all thought, or of concentrating the mind with the utmost intensity upon nothing in particular.
>
> Ordinarily it is a strange compound of exercises consisting of forced and painful postures, twisting and contortions of the limbs, and suppressions of the breath undertaken apparently with no object except to attain complete vacuity of mind.[1]

The most unnatural and painful postures are sometimes persisted in for years; the variety and intensity of the various forms of suffering which

[1] Williams, *Hind.*, pp. 200–201.

are thus self-inflicted would surpass belief if they were not attested by trustworthy witnesses. A Hindu priest advocating the practices of his cult on American soil admits that insanity is sometimes the result of the Yoga teaching. He says:

> Raja-yoga is stopping the functions of the mind's volitions. By volitions of the mind, are meant thought currents.
>
> By the practice of Raja-yoga, the outflow of these thought currents can be *entirely stopped* and turned inwards in one concentrated stream upon the soul.

He admonishes his devotees wishing to pursue the course to be sure and secure the services of a proper, and we may add, a well-paid, "guru." He says:

> An adept Yogi-guru, without whose help in every detail of it no student can attain the highest results, is very hard to be found. Many who now practise it under inexperienced gurus in India *meet with early death, or develop incurable diseases, or even turn insane!*

This fact has already been illustrated by sending back to their friends in America the hopelessly insane who went to India to study the theories and practices of Hinduism.

*Brahma.* Among the multitudinous gods of this period, the principal deities are Brahma, Shiva, and Vishnu. The first of these is said in the Code of Manu to have been the first male (Purusha) and to have been produced from the Supreme Self-existent Spirit:

> And Brahma, having divided his own substance, became half male and half female, and from that female was born Virag, and from Virag was born Manu, the second progenitor and producer of all beings.

Furthermore, he modestly (?) informs us: "The god Brahma, having formed this system of laws himself, taught it fully to me in the beginning!"[1]

In the Brahmanas, the only real entity had been brahman in the neuter gender, when impersonal; when he became masculine, he became the creator, and when manifested in the higher order of men, he was called Brahmana—the Brahmans. It is claimed that gods and men and demons were reconstructed from previous forms, and the bodies which Brahma abandoned became day, night, dawn, evening, etc.

> Afterward the hairs of Brahma which were shrivelled up fell from his head and became serpents. The creator of the world being incensed by the loss of his hair, created fierce beings who were denominated goblins—they were malignant fiends, and eaters of flesh. The divine Brahma then created birds from

[1] Manu, i., ii., 32.

his own vitality, sheep from his breast, cows from his side, horses, elephants, and other animals from his feet, whilst from the hairs of his body grew roots and herbs.[1]

This god is represented as having four faces, and either riding upon a swan, or closely accompanied by that bird. At the close of the enormous periods given as the sum of his life[2] Brahma himself expires, and with him the other gods, when everything in the world is resolved back into primary matter, or primary spirit, according to the different theories of the various philosophers.

*Shiva or Siva.*[3] Shiva ranks as the greatest ascetic and he is represented as sitting under a tree, while the canopy which covers him is formed of a serpent's head. There he remains motionless, and immovable, as the trunk of a tree, and rooted to the same spot for millions of years. He is the representative Yogi, and his Hindu devotees are

[1] Aitarea-brahmana, ii., 4–10.

[2] One day in the life of Brahma consists of 2,160,000,000 of years. At the end of this period, he sleeps, and then reconstructs the world. He lives one hundred of these days, which complete the life of Brahma.

[3] This name is usually written Siva, but in that case there should be a diacritical point on the first letter, giving it the sound of Sh. As these points have not been considered essential in the present volume, the name is here spelled as pronounced, the same rule being followed in the kindred appellations of Saivism, Sakti, Saktism, etc.

called Yogis, who worship him as the Supreme Being, and by the constant practice of Yoga they hope to attain union with this deity. The gods themselves are represented as having attained their position through the performance of rites and sacrifices. In the Satapatha-brahmana it is said:

> The gods lived constantly in fear of death—
> The mighty Ender; so with toilsome rites
> They worshipped and performed religious acts
> Till they became immortal.
> Then the Ender said to the gods,
> "As ye have made yourselves
> Imperishable, so will men endeavour
> To free themselves from me—what portion then
> Shall I possess in man?" The gods replied,
> "Henceforth no being shall become immortal
> In his own body; this his mortal frame
> Shalt thou seize; this shall remain thine own,
> This shall become perpetually thy food."[1]

Shiva was developed from Rudra, one of the storm-gods who rode in the train of Indra; as one of the manifestations of Brahma, he became the world-dissolver. His function of destroyer is interchangeable with that of creator, in which form he is worshipped throughout the Empire. In this character he is represented by the reproductive linga and it is estimated that there are more than twenty-eight millions of these stone objects of

[1] Satapatha-brahmana, Williams's trans.

worship in India.[1] He is sometimes represented as a naked ascetic with matted hair and his body covered with ashes, while again he is wild and jovial, fond of liquor and dancing, living in the Himalaya Mountains with his wife in various forms and surrounded by a group of grotesque attendants who, like their master, are excited by drink. The personal appearance of Shiva must be rather striking, as it is said his throat is black and his hair bright red; the number of his hands varies with different authorities, some claiming that he has four, while others insist that he has eight.

He has five faces, in one of which there is a third eye situated in the middle of the forehead. His garment is a tiger skin, while around his neck are two necklaces, one of them being made of human skulls, and the other of serpents which twist their horrible forms around his neck and body.

In fact he bristles everywhere with living snakes—he wears them as ornaments on his hands, they are bound in his long matted hair, they coil around his feet and legs, they hang like mammoth pendants from his ears, until he is like

> Gorgon rising from the infernal lakes,
> With horrors armed, and curls of hissing snakes.

[1] Sir Monier Monier-Williams, *Indian Wisdom*, p. 325.

He rides upon a white bull which is his constant companion. Four of the Puranas make Shiva the Supreme God and he enjoys a fame which reaches much farther back than that of Vishnu, the preserver. In the later Hindu scriptures he assumes a multitude of functions, each of them being indicated by one of his thousand and one names. Aside from the phallic worship which is the main feature of his dominance, to which allusion has already been made, the most important teaching of Shaivism is Yoga, its favourite philosophy.

Although the quotations and descriptions given above are taken from their own standard books, the Hindu priests in Europe and America are declaring:

> Shiva is the presiding Deity of the weal of creation, hence his name—Shiva. He is the conqueror and destroyer of darkness. He helps his devotees to dispel the darkness of ignorance generated in their minds by its Tama Attribute . . . and thus uncover its attribute of Sattwa by the illumination of which their souls reach the state of Moksha—freedom from the bondage of matter—and finally merge into the Divine Essence whence it originally sprang.

Thus do they misrepresent the teaching of their own sacred books for the sake of winning converts and getting Anglo-Saxon gold into their possession.

*Ceremonies.* Dr. Rajandra-lala Mitra is the native authority for the following description of the services at the great Shiva temple in Orissa. Shiva is here worshipped under the form of his symbol, which is a large uncarved block of granite, about eight feet long, but which is partly buried in the ground; the daily devotion here consists of no less than twenty-two ceremonial acts:

(1) At the first appearance of the dawn, bells are rung to arouse the deity from his slumbers.

(2) A lamp with many wicks is waved in front of the stone.

(3) The god's teeth are cleaned by pouring water on the symbol.

(4) The god is bathed by pouring several pitchers full of water on the stone.

(5) He is dressed by putting clothes on the symbol.

(6) His first breakfast is offered, consisting of grain, sweetmeats, and curds, besides cocoanuts.

(7) Shiva has his principal breakfast, when cakes and more substantial viands are served.

(8) A light lunch is offered.

(9) He has his regular lunch.

(10) The midday dinner is served, consisting of curry, rice, pastry, cakes, cream, etc., while the priest waves a many-flamed lamp and burns incense before the stone.

(11) Strains of discordant music rouse the god from his afternoon nap at four o'clock, the temple

having been closed during the preceding hours in order to give him an opportunity to sleep.

(12) Sweetmeats are offered.

(13) The afternoon bath is administered.

(14) He is dressed as in the morning.

(15) Another meal is served.

(16) Another bath is administered.

(17) The full dress ceremony takes place, when costly vestments are placed upon the stone, with yellow flowers, and p-rfumery.

(18) Another offering of food is presented.

(19) After an interval of an hour, another meal.

(20) Five masks and a damaru are brought in. The masks represent the five faces of Shiva, and the damaru is a sort of rattle or drum, shaped like an hour-glass. The god is supposed to use this as a musical instrument while dancing.

(21) The waving of lights is again performed just before bedtime.

(22) A bedstead is brought in, and Shiva is ready for his night's rest.[1]

This daily performance by a corps of priests is one form of worship, but this is comparatively innocent, and that cannot be said of all of them, for just as the Vaishnavas worship ten male incarnations of Vishnu, so the Shaktas worship ten female manifestations of Shiva, or rather of his Shakti or energy.

On his return from India, President Barrows of

[1] Rajandra-lala Mitra, vol. ii. of his work on Orissa.

Oberlin testified that mothers bring their young daughters to the temples of Shiva and there dedicate them to a life of shame in his service.

"The Shivite cult," says Bhattacharya, "is the most common and ancient form of abomination worship."[1] See also this author's description of the horrible rites practised by various sects of Yoga, Aghoris, Shaktas, or Tantriks, all of which are different forms of Shiva worship.

The Aghoris and Panthi Yogis profess to carry to its logical sequence the Vedanta philosophy which was so highly eulogised in America by Vivekananda, and they claim that eating human flesh which has reached the stage of putrefaction will give them a knowledge of magic. There is a Gujerati work called Agama-prakasa, the author of which asserts that there are instances of these devotees eating corpses which are stolen from the Mohammedan burying-grounds, and that the head of the Aghoris sect living near Siddhapur, subsists upon scorpions, lizards, and loathesome insects which have been left to partial decay in the skulls of dead men.[2]

> The fact is [says the learned Brahman] that as Brahmanism inculcated cleanliness and the eating of

[1] Bhatt., *Hindu Castes and Sects*, pp. 368–9.

[2] Quoted by Williams, *Brah. and Hind.*, pp. 87–94.

wholesome food, the Aghoris, who formed one of the sects setting up 'opposition shops' as it were, insisted upon the utmost degree of filth and hoped to get alms by horrifying the people, and not by getting their respect.[1]

The British Government of course is not encouraging this sort of thing. For instance we have a record of one of them by the name of Krishna Das Babaji who was fined fifteen rupees by Mr. Ishan Chandra Sen, Deputy Magistrate of Berhampore, for committing a public nuisance, by devouring part of a woman's corpse in the presence of a company of people at a burning ghat. Some of the Aghori-panthis claim that if, at initiation, they refuse to eat dead men's flesh, they would be dismissed by the guru as unfit for their calling. Convictions and fines have made these offensive creatures much less intrusive upon the public, and it is believed that their numbers are happily decreasing. "Yet many may still be found, who believe they are propitiating Shiva, not by worship, but by feeding upon filth and offal of all kinds."[2]

*The Tantras.* These books are listed in the seventh division of the enumeration of the nine

[1] Bhattacharya, *Hindu Castes and Sects*, pp. 393–394.

[2] Williams, *Brah. and Hind.*, pp. 87–94.

canonical scriptures and the majority are more modern than the Puranas, although some of them may have been contemporaneous with a portion of that enormous series.

They have never been fully translated into English, but some unhappy scholar of the future may be obliged to examine the loathsome pages more fully than has as yet been done. The nauseous taste repelled even the self-sacrificing industry of Burnouf when he found them to be as immoral as they are absurd.

A Brahman writing from Calcutta says:

> The Tantras recommending human sacrifice are accepted as authority by the Brahmans of almost all classes throughout India. Yet in practice, the only animals usually sacrificed by the Shakti worshippers in Northern India re the sheep and the goat.

He might have added that the credit of nearly putting an end to human sacrifice in India belongs to the British Government. Nevertheless the crime is sometimes committed in remote districts and Crooke mentions significant instances of the kind as having taken place during the last few years.[1]

"The Tantrik and the Shivite cults being equally

[1] W. Crooke, B.A., of the Bengal Civil Service, *Pop. Rel. and Folk-Lore of Northern India*, vol. ii., p. 171.

indecent, their gurus cannot ordinarily explain their true nature."[1]

> Shaktism, [says Williams], is devotion to the wives of Shiva as impersonations of the forces of nature in female form. . . . It might be expected that a creed like this would be likely to degenerate into various forms of licentiousness on the one hand and witchcraft on the other. But if such consequences might be expected, the actual fact has been worse than could be foretold by the most gloomy pessimist. . . . In Shaktism we are confronted with the worst possible results, and the most superstitious ideas, that have disgraced and degraded the human race. As the most conspicuous god of the Puranas is Vishnu with his incarnations, so the most prominent deity of the Tantras is Shiva in his manifestations, especially in the innumerable forms of his female counterparts.
>
> It must not be forgotten, however, that there are a few Tantras which substitute Radha, the first wife of Krishna, for Durga or Kali, the wife of Shiva.[2]

And yet this cult has been successfully introduced into both Europe and America. In the United States, the initiates are under the care of five gurus, one of whom calls himself "Om, the Omnipotent," and flourished financially in New York until his headquarters were closed by the police, when he was compelled to seek his victims in other cities.

*Kali, the Wife of Shiva.* Some confusion has

[1] Bhatt., *Hind. Castes and Sects*, pp. 87, 451–452.

[2] Williams, *Brah. and Hind.*, pp. 189–190.

obtained on this subject from the fact that Shiva had several wives, but the goddess who is adored on American soil as the "Conqueress of Time and the Door of Eternity" is Kali, who is worshipped in Bengal under the name of Durga, where she rides upon a tiger, but at Calcutta and Benares she is the veritable goddess of destruction and she is terrible indeed. As to the personal appearance of this deity, the following is a free translation by Williams of two passages in the Tantras:

> A Kaulika [worshipper of Kali, or Shakti] should worship Kali who lives among dead bodies; who is terrible and has fearful aws; who has uncombed hair and a glowing tongue; who constantly drinks blood—who has four hands, and a splendid garland formed of the heads of the giants she has slain, and whose blood she has drunk—who has a sword in her lotus hand—who is fearless and awards blessings. . . .
>
> She is black as the large clouds and has the whole sky for her clothes. She has a string of skulls around her neck, and her throat is besmeared with blood. She wears earrings consisting of two dead bodies; she has terrible teeth, and a smiling face, her form is awful and she dwells in the burning grounds for the consuming of corpses.[1]

According to Bhattacharya, this description is exceedingly mild. He claims that the symbolism

[1] Williams, *Brah. and Hind.* pp., 198–199.

attached to this dreadful figure is vastly worse than any picture of the idol can possibly be. He says:

> The true nature of such images is not generally known, though it is defined in unmistakable terms in the Dhyan, or formula for contemplating the goddess Kali. . . . What its real meaning is, cannot possibly be explained here. Those inclined to dive into such filth must study the ritual for Kali worship.[1]

This goddess who thirsts for human blood is worshipped with the same revolting ceremonies as when she is adored and propitiated under the name of Durga.

*Modern Devotees.* Although this description of Kali is taken from their own official text-books, and although Hindus themselves admit that the pen-picture is a small part of the truth, still white women are being taught to invoke this horrible myth as "The good mother of all the suffering ones of earth!" If Anglo-Saxons are desirous of invoking "Kali, Mother Kali," the only proper place to do so is in her own temple at Benares, a brief description of which will be found in the following chapter. Let them bring their offerings of money and flowers to this shrine where a vivid

[1] Bhatt., p. 408.

representation of the goddess is reeking with the stench of putrefying blood, and there piously invoke "Kali, Mother Kali!"

Availing themselves of the profound ignorance of their devotees on this subject, the gurus in America are declaring that:

> Without Durga, his Shakti (energy), Shiva is inert; with his Shakti, he is alive and rules the universe. . . . Durga is the highest spiritual phase of Kali—Conqueress of Time and Door of Eternity. . . . Her devotees, called *Shaktas* (Shakti worshippers), meditate upon her as the Great Mother, and *pray to her* for her grace. . . . They are helped to Moskha, or led into the path of Krishna; this last is the greatest of all her gifts.

An Englishwoman who is now a nun of the Rama-Krishna order was summoned from India to America to exercise especial supervision over a rich woman and her money, lest some traces of reason might be revived in her enfeebled mind. This keeper of the diseased and infatuated woman kept her own daughter away from the bedside of the patient, and after her death, the cult through its representatives made a fight in the courts for her fortune, but were fortunately defeated. But this Englishwoman who thus became the willing tool of the Hindu priest not only performs her daily acts of devotion before the picture or image of a heathen deity, but says her prayers to "Kali, the Divine Mother!" concerning whose beauties and glories she has written a book!

# CHAPTER IV

## MODERN HINDUISM

Phases of Idolatry. Temples of Shiva. Shrine of Kali. Temples of Vishnu. Demons and Devils. Hanuman, the Monkey God. Serpent Worship. Other Sacred Animals. Deified Trees and Plants. Position of Widows. Panditi Ramabai.

THERE is no proof of the existence of idolatry during the Vedic period, and it does not appear to have prevailed very extensively at the time of the early compilation of the Code of Manu, although it is there declared that the accidental breaker of images shall repair them, and also pay a fine. The pandits insist that there was no idolatry in India until it was introduced by the Buddhists. It is certain, however, that Hinduism has assigned no limits to the ever-increasing number of its gods, many of whom are represented by thousands of figures, so the idol census of India can be only guesswork. Even rough stones which are supposed to have fallen from heaven are among the objects of adoration, and frequently have temples or shrines built above them. Small pebbles found in rivers are often reverenced, and they are held to be pervaded by the presence of deity and need no consecration. Artificial idols, on the other hand, are consecrated with a long ceremony called "endowing with breath," and until this is done they are not objects of worship.

*Temples of Shiva.* Benares is especially noted as a sacred city. It is described as having been separated from the world by the Creator and placed upon one of the points of Shiva's trident; consequently it is crowded with shrines and idols. Not only this but sacred bulls jostle against the visitor in the streets, and impudent monkeys make free with his belongings, while everywhere images, symbols, holy wells and trees intrude upon his vision. There are about two thousand temples here, in a city of something more than 200,000 inhabitants, and it is estimated that at least half a million idols receive the adoration and the offerings of the multitude. Shiva is the favourite deity with the upper classes (as Krishna is of the others), and among the millions of his stone symbols, many have shrines built above them. Beside one of his temples at Benares there is the "holy well of knowledge" where it is said the idol voluntarily took refuge when his house was destroyed by the

Mohammedan invaders. This well is the constant resort of devotees who throw into its depths offerings of rice and flowers, until the putrid condition of the water makes the whole neighbourhood intolerable. But still a Brahman is constantly employed in drawing up the loathsome fluid which is called "the water of purification," and selling it to the crowds, who gladly pay a large price and eagerly drink it, in order that the foul water may cleanse their fouler souls![1]

There are said to be one thousand and eight temples of Shiva in India (one for each of his names), and of these the most important is the great structure near the celebrated rock of Trichinopoly which has been dedicated to him as "The Lord of the Jambu Tree."

This shrine has many beautiful colonnades and pillars, while in the central court there is a large column of metal from which a flag is flung to the breeze, and near it is the tree over which the god is supposed to preside. In other temples he is worshipped as "The Peerless Lord of the Mango

[1] Having quite recently returned to Oxford after spending a winter in India and China, Prof. A. H. Sayce in a personal letter to the author says: "Hinduism has its centre at Benares, which is a nightmare of disgusting horrors. One of the most eminent archæologists in India said to me: 'India has no art, no history, and no industries of its own.' That is most true, and must remain true as long as Hinduism exists."

Tree"; in another as "Lord of the Vata Tree" or banyan; in a shrine in the south of Vindhya he is adored as "Lord of the Vineyard."

*Shrine of Kali.* It is also at Benares that we find the elaborate temple which is dedicated to Kali, the favourite wife of Shiva. Judge Henry Austin, who has recently visited Benares, and the famous temple of Kali, or Durga, gives a graphic description of this place of worship as seen by an eye-witness. He says:

> It is sometimes called the Monkey Temple on account of the multitudes of repulsive monkeys that swarm there; they have become impudent from over-kindness and unhealthy from overeating.
>
> Within the temple, the centre of attention is the shrine of Kali, a bloodthirsty she-demon whose thirst must be quenched daily. She loomed up as a hideous black figure with distorted face and open mouth, her tongue hanging to the waist line. About her body, huge serpents writhed and at her throat was a necklace of human skulls.
>
> Idols of this engaging creature are in every village in India, but the centre of her cult is Benares. There in the court occur the daily sacrifices to her, which, thanks to the British rule, no longer consist in decapitating young children.
>
> Kali must now be satisfied with the blood of a goat that is killed by the same method that the children were. The goat is stretched forward and a priest

severs the animal's head with a single stroke of a sharp knife, then the hot blood is smeared upon the faces of the priests before they go into the presence of Kali, to pour the warm blood over her malodorous figure. Unless this is done daily, she will bring pestilence and famine upon the land.

Usually the head of the goat alone is taken to the goddess and the blood-stained priests dance about the body chanting weird songs, while hundreds of grey mangy monkeys chatter at them from their perches on the porticoes, window ledges, and elsewhere. In times of famine, the goat is not enough for Kali, and one of the great water buffaloes is brought in and decapitated.[1]

And yet, this very goddess, reeking with the stench of decaying blood, is eulogised in Europe and America as "the Divine Mother"! White women are being taught that this loathsome myth "holds the key of the gate of Goloka, Krishna's Abode of Love bliss"!

*Temples of Vishnu.* These are abundant all over the country; the best known of them being that of Jagan-nath at Puri in Orissa, where the images of Krishna with those of his brother, and sister are found. Major-General Cunningham, who so ably conducted the Archæological Survey of India, has demonstrated that these three images

[1] Judge Austin, *New England Magazine*, vol. xliii., May, p. 17.

in the Jagan-nath temple were derived from the three combined emblems of the Buddhist Trinatra.

The most elaborate shrine of Vaishnavism is the Sri-rangam located on an island of that name in the river Kaveri. It might be called a city within itself as hundreds of Brahmans live there, and multitudes of pilgrims throng the streets. It is composed of seven great enclosures, one within the other, the theory being that each bulwark of massive walls includes a court of increasing sanctity, until the devotees shall reach the centre where the great idol lies in state. Every surrounding wall has openings filled with ponderous gates, each gateway being surmounted by a tower. The vast structure has cost millions of dollars in construction, and other millions in maintenance.

The original idol of Vishnu is supposed to be immovable, but another image has been constructed and consecrated. On festal days it is placed in an enormous car, one of which is connected with every Vaishnava temple, and is dragged through the streets by thousands of men. The jewelry and decorations of even this secondary figure have cost a fabulous amount of money. The great idol crown alone is estimated at 80,000 rupees, while the breastplate, necklace, and other ornaments are worth as much more.

*Demons and Devils.* These terms are by no means interchangeable, as many demons are more or less friendly to humanity, while devils are always malicious. There are legions of them—lying devils, gambling devils, thieving devils, and so on through the list of evil spirits which lie in wait for the weak-minded and thoughtless in order to induce them to commit crimes. In the south of India, demonophobia is especially prevalent. Every village has its own especial evil spirits and people are always exposed to their attacks. Fortunately, however, each community has also its own tutelary divinities, but these must be propitiated for their good offices, while the devils must be placated as far as possible by offerings and oblations. The ceremonies of these worshippers are very long and tedious, as well as expensive. Various forms of devil worship are, appropriately enough, associated with that of Shiva, his consort Kali, and their two sons. Among the demons also there are some who are greatly feared, one of them being called Kanara; this is a terrible pig-faced goblin who was created, it is said, by the curse of Shiva when he denounced some young pigs that devastated his garden, and they were thereupon collectively transformed into a single malicious demon. A goodly revenue is derived by the priesthood from the sale of devil stones, which are taken home and used as talismans against evil spirits.

*Hanuman, the Monkey God.* Not only are the temples of Shiva and Vishnu crowded with idols, but even the heroes of the great epics receive their full share of offerings. One of the most popular of these is the monkey ally of Rama in the story of the Rama-yana. He was called the son of the wind and could assume any form at pleasure. He could tear up great trees by the roots or even lift mountains from their foundations and carry them through the air, or handle those which the other monkeys in Rama's army brought to him to build the wonderful bridge at Ceylon upon which Rama's troops crossed over to the other side. He it was, also, who made a complete reconnoissance of the enemy's stronghold by assuming the form of a cat, and finally in his own form of a monkey destroyed the orchards and burned the palaces of the foe.[1] He will always be a popular figure in Indian mythology and his images are covered with red paint—the sacred vermilion; they are numerous in many localities.

In the great temple just outside of the town of

[1] Reed's *Hindu Literature*, pp. 161–271.

Kaira, which is devoted to the worship of Hanuman, offerings of oil are constantly presented to the god. Within his enclosure, are shrines to both Rama and Krishna, but they occupy only subordinate positions. There is also a shrine to the goddess of smallpox, and around it a cloister which is used as a lodging-place for travellers. Not only are divine honours paid to Hanuman, but all his kith and kin of the monkey tribe are held sacred, and they are everywhere undisturbed. They make havoc with the clothing of visitors, and keep the temples filthy; they sometimes tear off the roofs of the native houses, apparently merely for amusement, but no owner would dare drive them away, whatever damages they might do upon the premises.

*Serpent Worship.* Among reptiles the snake is the most sacred, and his immunity from injury costs the people much loss and suffering. During 1904, nearly ten thousand head of cattle (9994) were killed by snake bite, and the habit of walking barefoot makes the number of human victims unnecessarily large. During the same year 21,827 men, women, and children died in agony in consequence of the attacks of these deified reptiles. These are official figures, and of course not nearly all of the cases were reported to the King's officers. Good authorities estimate the total deaths from snake bite in India at 25,000 annually and some claim the number will reach 40,000.

Mr. Walhouse says:

> One of the highest mountains in the South Kanara Ghats has a celebrated serpent temple where great numbers of the 'coiling folk' reside in holes and crevices which have been made for them.
>
> To propitiate these creatures, people who have made vows roll along serpent fashion, and some will even roll their bodies up to the temple from the foot of the hill, half a mile distant. They also take home with them portions of earth from the sacred serpent holes; this is believed to cure leprosy if rubbed on the parts affected; it will also cure barrenness if a little be put into the mouth daily. Serpentine body wriggling is also practised farther south where small snake temples are common.[1]

In Southern India it is a fixed article of faith that all who have killed a snake, especially a cobra, will, either in this life or the next, be punished with leprosy, barrenness, or ophthalmia. Therefore it behooves all who are thus afflicted in this life to visit snake shrines and conciliate the serpent gods.

There is one festival in which women—

[1] Walhouse, *Ind. Ant.* vol. vii., Feb.

"Wives of the Snake"—go round begging for the Brahmans, and in a Bengal festival the men march entwined with serpents, while the chief man has a roc-boa round his neck, and is carried, or rides upon a buffalo.[1]

*Other Sacred Animals.* Especial reverence is also accorded to many other animals for various reasons. While serpents are associated with both Shiva and Vishnu, Brahma is attended by a goose or swan, while the elephant belongs to Indra. Yama rides a buffalo and Agni a ram. Kamadeva, the god of love, is attended by a parrot, Ganesa by a rat, and Varuna by a fish. All of these therefore are entitled to especial consideration. But the most sacred of all animals are those of the cattle kind and especially the cow. Each portion of her body is inhabited by some deity and every hair is inviolable. A Brahman told a story of a celebrated saint who was compelled to commit suicide by drowning as a penalty for accidentally swallowing the hair of a cow while drinking her milk. And even this punishment was not sufficient as he was obliged afterward to undergo the penalty of being born a Mohammedan.

[1] James Fergusson, *Tree and Serpent Worship*, p. 257. See also *Shakti Ceremonies in India*, p. 558 *seq.*

President Barrows of Oberlin College said that he had seen the natives crawling on their hands and knees through the filth of the barnyard in order to approach a cow with proper humility, and then kiss her tail! All excreta from a cow is hallowed, and the ground which it touches is a consecrated spot, while the urine is the most effective of all holy waters and cleanses all who partake of it.

The Code of Manu, the great judicial authority, from the decrees of which there is no appeal, says:

> Eating for one day of the excrement and urine of a cow mixed with milk, curds, and clarified butter, and water boiled with Kusa grass, and fasting for a day and a night, is the penance called Santapana.[1]

The *panca-gavya* penance consists in swallowing the five products of the cow as given above, without fasting, or the Kusa grass solution. This is declared to be "a sufficient atonement for having stolen food, a carriage, bed, chair, roots, flowers, or fruits."[2] This is said to be the penance which Vivekananda had to undergo on his return to India, after feasting luxuriously on American beef. Of course the killing of a cow is criminal, and Manu decrees that "the guilty man shall make atonement by attending upon a herd of cattle, guarding them from all injury, following

[1] Manu, bk. xi., 212. [2] Bk xi., 165.

them night and day in all weathers for three months, and swallowing the dust which is raised by their feet."[1] Images of cows are sold in the bazars and bought as objects of reverence. The letting loose of a bull properly stamped with the symbol of Shiva, in sacred cities, like Gaya and Benares, so that the stray animal may be tended and fed by the populace, is a highly meritorious act.

*Deified Trees and Plants.* Not only animals, but many trees and plants are supposed to be permeated with divinity. Perhaps the tulasi, or holy basil is the most revered. It is sacred to Vishnu and prayers are often offered to it, as if it were itself a goddess. Women perform many "meritorious acts" by walking around this shrub, which is carefully cultivated. As animals, especially monkeys, are sometimes made to go through the marriage ceremony, so also the wedding of the tulasi to the idol of Krishna takes place once every year, in the month Kartik, in nearly every Hindu family. The bilva (*Ægle marmelos*), sometimes called the wood apple, is dedicated to Shiva, its triple leaves being constantly placed upon his symbol. The banyan tree, which mul-

[1] Manu, bk. xi., 108–115.

tiplies itself by sending its branches downward, is sacred to Kala, or Time; this and the pipal, or pipalla, are supposed to represent immortality. The pipal (*Ficus religiosa*), sometimes called the bo-tree is the one under which Buddha finally attained to that state of mind called "perfect enlightenment." And this is regarded with especial sanctity by his followers. Tradition says that Gautama once directed Ananda to break off a branch of the tree under which he attained to Buddhahood, and plant it in the garden. "He who worships it," said Gautama, "will receive the same reward as if he worshipped me." Whether this be true or not, the Brahmans insist that he struggled hard to be worshipped as a god. They say: "He put an end to the old dynasty of kings, not for giving liberty to the people, but only to step into the throne himself, under a new name."[1] This tree must however have been highly reverenced in India before Buddha's time for it was regarded as being occupied by Brahma, and it is now sometimes invested with the sacred thread as if it were a real person. All the ceremonies of the Upanayana are then performed over it. The pipal is necessarily banished from the business districts however, as the Hindu is afraid to tell a

[1] Bhatt., p. 543.

lie under the shade of its branches. The arka plant is sacred to Surya, the sun, and the shami, or acacia is a goddess on her own account, and is supposed to contain fire. The superstition regarding trees has a wonderfully good effect upon the forestry of the country, because the natives are not only afraid to destroy any of the sacred trees or shrubs, but the planting of others adds greatly to the "merit" of the individual thus occupied.

*Position of Widows.* Even under the best circumstances we cannot expect the position of woman to be a very exalted one, in a country where the wife is declared to be "the marital property" of her husband and is therefore classed with "female camels, slave girls, she goats, and ewes."[1]

Marriages being concluded in many cases without the consent of either party, there is little chance for conjugal affection, but it is nevertheless true that a wife may sometimes be found who has little cause for complaint, except in the absence of freedom of thought and action; and she scarcely misses these, having been always accustomed to a condition of bondage. But however comfortable she may have been during her married life, every-

[1] See Manu, bk. iv., 48–51.

thing is changed in case she happens to survive her husband. It is understood that her widowhood is the penalty visited upon her for some fearful crime which she committed in a former birth, and her so-called friends consider it their duty to add what they can to her sufferings.

There is hardly a class of living beings whose wretched condition appeals more strongly to the humane man or woman than the widows of India. Very few people in Europe or America have even the remotest idea of the miseries which the Hindu woman must endure after the death of her husband. Manu, the great lawgiver whose rules are inviolable, enjoins the following duties upon her: "Let her emaciate her body by living voluntarily upon pure flowers, and fruits, but let her not, when her lord is dead, even pronounce the name of another man."[1] Perhaps even Manu would have hesitated about making such a decree had he known it would be the source of such indescribable suffering to millions of human beings. Devendra N. Das, an accomplished native scholar, writes on this subject as follows:

> The widow who has no parents has to pass her whole life under the roof of her father-in-law, and then she knows no comfort whatever. She has to meet from

[1] Manu, bk. v., 767.

her late husband's relations only unkind looks and unjust reproaches. She has to work like a slave, and for the reward of all her drudgery, she receives only hatred and abhorrence from her mother-in-law and her sisters-in-law. If there is disorder in the domestic arrangements of the family, the widow is blamed and cursed for it. . . . Even death cannot save a widow from indignities, for when a wife dies, she is burned in the clothes she had on, but a widow's corpse is covered with a coarse white cloth, and there is little ceremony at her funeral. . . .

"The English have abolished Sati [suttee] but alas! neither the English nor the angels know what goes on in our houses, and the Hindus not only do not care, but think it good!"

Such were the words of a widow, and well she might exclaim "neither the English nor the angels know," for Hindu as I am, I can vouch for her statement that very few Hindus have a fair knowledge of the actual sufferings of the widows among them, and fewer still care to know of the evils and horrors of the barbarous custom which victimises their own sisters and daughters in so ruthless a manner; nay, on the contrary, the majority of orthodox Hindus consider the practice good and salutary.[1]

*Pandita Ramabai.* This brave woman is still striving to take care of her large family of child-widows, and she pathetically laments the enforced and constant humiliation of the womanhood of her

[1] Devendra N. Das, *Nineteenth Century*, vol. xx., pp. 364-373.

country. She claims that the Aryan Hindus did indeed honour women and quotes some of the early precepts of the infallible Code in support of her position. But it must be remembered that the compilation of the Code of Manu has covered many years, and it would appear that this is the only explanation of the contradictory decrees and declarations there found concerning the treatment to be accorded to woman.

For instance Manu declares:

> Women must be honoured and adorned by their fathers, brothers, husbands, and brothers-in-law, who desire their own welfare. Where women are honoured the gods are pleased, but where they are not honoured, no sacred rite yields reward.[1]

But elsewhere and in a later volume it is said:

> Though destitute of virtue, or seeking pleasure elsewhere, or devoid of good qualities, yet a husband must be constantly worshipped as a god by a faithful wife.[2]

This and many other decrees of a similar nature made this educated Hindu woman say:

> Those who diligently and impartially read Sanskrit literature in the original cannot fail to recognise the lawgiver Manu as one of those hundreds who have done their best to make woman a hateful being in the world's eye. . . . She is forbidden to read the

[1] Manu, bk. iii., 55–56.

[2] Manu, bk. ix., 154.

(Hindu) sacred scriptures, she has no right to pronounce a single syllable out of them. . . . She, the loving mother of the nation, the devoted wife, the tender sister and affectionate daughter, is never fit for independence, and is "as impure as falsehood itself." I can say, honestly and truthfully, that I have never read any sacred book in Sanskrit literature, without meeting this kind of hateful sentiment about women. True they contain, here and there, a kind word about them, but such words seem to me a heartless mockery after having charged them, as a class, with crime and evil deeds. Profane literature is by no means less severe or more respectful towards women.[1]

Pandita is anxious to come to the United States again, and raise her voice against the deceptions which are being practised here by the Hindu priests. In a letter intended for publication she says:

What has shocked me most has been the report that there are women in America who are confessedly studying and adopting the philosophy of the Hindus. As I was born and educated in this philosophy, having taken my degree of Pandita in it, I am acquainted with both its literature, and its influence on my people, and I want to bear witness against its degradation. . . . It is all very nice to read pretty translations where much that is degrading has been expurgated, but the original is quite another thing.

[1] Pandita Ramabai, *High Caste Hindu Woman*, pp. 81–82.

Not only this, but she calls attention to the enforced position of woman under the influence of such teaching. She says of the Hindu woman:

After rising early and attending to the cares of her house, her next duty is to put her head on the sacred feet of her husband and worship him. . . . The philosophy of India teaches that there are five sinless lies, and among them are the lies told to women. If American women think they would like such philosophy, India is the best place for the study of the *results* of Hinduism.

# CHAPTER V

## PRESENT CONDITIONS

Vaishnavism. Ten Incarnations. Bala-Rama. Krishna Vasudeva. Wives of Krishna. Death of the God.

AS the followers of Shiva centralised their creed into a system known as Shaivism, so also the doctrine of the later sect is called Vaishnavism. These schools were stimulated into activity by the Brahmans, who needed new forces in order to conquer Buddhism. During the Middle Ages when the Puranas were written there was fierce rivalry between the adherents of Shiva and Vishnu; now, however, it is asserted that any one can be a worshipper of either without ignoring the other, and hence they dwell together in comparative peace.

Vaishnavism is sometimes a form of monotheism with Vishnu as supreme, especially as he is represented in the later incarnations of Rama and Krishna. But like other forms of Hinduism it is most elastic in its ideas, being quite capable of adaptation to almost any other creed when it seems politic to do so. It has no formal confession of faith, but it has a series of eighteen Puranas, some of which extol one god, and some another, and each of these books may be used as an authority for almost any one of their theories.

The later system includes Brahmanism by claiming: "There is one Being and no second," and also their oft-repeated assertion that there are many deities, or many forms of one. Like Shaivism it enjoins asceticism and austerities, even while like Shaktism or Tantrism it gives unbridled rein to self-indulgence. Like Buddhism it preaches liberty, equality, and fraternity, especially endorsing the humane treatment of all animals and reptiles, on the ground that either of them may be a new form which is being worn by a dead priest, or a departed relative. Like Buddhism, too, it fails to include in its humane category the women and children of India.

Vaishnavism even looks upon Christianity with some degree of condescension while winning Anglo-Saxon funds—sometimes claiming that it is a development of their own religion which is suited to Europeans and Americans! Their halls in the United States are decorated with mottoes indicating that Christianity and Vaishnavism are virtually one and the same thing! We have a Vishnu in the early songs, but there he is merely a secondary representation of solar energy. The Hindus themselves admit that Vishnu as a deity is a comparatively modern creation, although Prof. Bhandarkar, Vice-Chancellor of the Bombay University, claims: "The ten Incarnations of Vishnu had become quite an ordinary article of belief in A.D. 1014, and Buddha had been admitted into the popular pantheon."[1] It was centuries later than this, however, before the Vishnu Purana was written, according to the best Oriental scholars.

*Ten Incarnations.* The idea of this divinity was expanded and spread into various ramifications. He is represented as having undergone nine different avatars, or descents, and is expected to undergo the tenth in future. In the Bhagavata-purana, these are multiplied into twenty-two, while in some of the others there are twenty-four or even twenty-eight, but the number commonly received is the original ten.

Bhagwanlal R. Badshah admits: "This doctrine may have been originally started to check

[1] Prof. Bhandarkar, *Trans. Ninth Internat. Congress of Orientalists*, vol. i., p. 426.

the progress of Buddhism, and to reorganise Brahmanism."[1] It is true there were older legends of the fish and some other forms in the combination, but all scholars, both Hindu and Anglo-Saxon, admit that the ten incarnations were not developed until the Puranic period, and they were then as now in the following order:

(1) *Matsya, the Fish.* In this shape, Vishnu saved Manu from the deluge. This legend is found in several of the sacred books and will be considered later.

(2) *Kurma, the Tortoise.* In this form Vishnu went down into the ocean to recover the lost nectar of the gods, and other valuables which had been lost in the flood. In this beautiful legend the gods are represented as having been conquered in battle by demons, and robbed of their strength, whereupon Vishnu gave orders to have the ocean churned into a nectar for the gods, declaring that this would restore their power and enable them to destroy their enemies. The gods were therefore ordered to collect all plants and herbs, and cast them into the sea, taking the mountain Mandara for a churning stick, and Vasuki the serpent for a rope, while Vishnu himself in the form of a colossal tortoise became a resting place for the mountain.

[1] Badshah, *Ninth Internat. Cong. of Orientalists*, vol. i., p. 134.

Then they churned the ocean until they produced the ambrosial food of immortality.

(3) *Varaha, the Boar.* Vishnu descended in the shape of an enormous boar to deliver the world from the power of the golden-eyed demon. The Vishnu-purana describes this animal as being one thousand yojanas, or forty-five hundred miles, in height, and ten yojanas, or forty-five miles, in breadth.

> He had the colour of a dark cloud; his roar was like thunder; his bulk, vast as a mountain; his tusks white, sharp, and fearful. Fire flashed from his eyes like lightning, and he was radiant as the sun. His shoulders were round, fat, and large, and he strode along like a powerful lion.[1]

Only a few years since one of the finest literary men in India began a paper with an invocation to "The Heavenly Boar!" Scholars have called attention to the fact that the first three incarnations of Vishnu were all connected with the tradition of a universal deluge.

(4) *Nara-Sinha, the Man-Lion.* This was the form chosen by Vishnu in which to deliver the world from the tyranny of an evil spirit who had obtained from Brahma a promise that he should not be slain either by a god, a man, or an animal.

[1] Vishnu-purana, Wilson's trans., p. 31.

(5) *Vamana, the Dwarf.* This character was assumed to deprive the demon Bali of the dominion of the three worlds. Vishnu presented himself as a very diminutive man, and solicited as much land as he could step over in three paces. When this request was granted he strode over heaven, and earth, but in compassion to the demon he left hell in his possession.

(6) *Parsu-Rama, or Bala-Rama.* Rama with the axe. In this character, Vishnu is said to have cleared the earth of the military class twenty-one times.

(7) *Rama-Chandra.* This was the hero of the beautiful story of the Ramayana, one of the two great Hindu epics. This colossal poem is so sacred that

> Whoever reads or hears the Ramayana will be freed from all sin. Those who read or hear it for the sake of riches will certainly acquire wealth. . . . The Ramayana heals diseases, removes all fear of enemies, compensates for the loss of wealth or fame, prevents loss of life, and secures all that is desired.

(8) *Krishna—the Dark God.* The younger brother of Bala-Rama, the strong Rama, has sometimes been called the eighth avatar instead of Krishna, but in later times the younger brother appears to have supplanted him.

(9) *Buddha*. According to the Brahmans, Vishnu assumed this form to delude the demons into neglecting the worship of the gods and thus expose themselves to punishment.

(10) *Kalki or Kalkin*. This is the future manifestation when the god will come forth on a white horse with a drawn sword in his hand, for the final destruction of the world. This last picture from the Vishnu-purana may have been drawn from the book of Revelation.[1]

In his paper before the Congress of Orientalists held in London, B. R. Badshah claims that this incarnation represents the British Government. He says:

> This prophecy has now already been fulfilled. This age of art and inventions has reference to the British rule in India. Kalki is described as riding a white horse: a white horse means a white-skinned race. . . . There are grounds for this exposition, as the people of India twenty years ago were speaking of the British Government as a Rama-raja, that is a godly government. As deifications are comparisons, this comparison will soon be sanctioned universally as a deification.[2]

*Rama*. The gallant hero of the Ramayana who was the seventh avatar of Vishnu was given the

[1] Rev. xix., 11–16.

[2] *Trans.*, vol. i p. 139.

additional name of Chandra when he was placed among the incarnations.

The ten-headed demon Ravanna had secured a promise from Brahma that he should not be slain by either gods, demons, or genii. This assurance had been gained by long austerities on the part of the demon, who had stood upon his head in the midst of five fires for ten thousand years. After obtaining the coveted promise, his conduct became so outrageous that the other gods came to Vishnu praying that he might deliver them from this mighty power for evil. The great Vishnu was gracious to his noble petitioners and answered:

> Be no longer alarmed: your foe shall fall at my feet. Ravanna in his pride of power did not ask Brahma to preserve him from men or monkeys, for he deemed them beneath his notice. But I will take advantage of this omission and cause his destruction by the very means which he despises. I will myself be born as Rama, you shall assist me by assuming the form of monkeys, and together we will overthrow this terrible enemy of gods and men.

Afterward, Ravanna carried off by force Sita, the lovely bride of the banished prince, and was followed long by the frantic husband, before he met with a host of monkeys under the leadership of Hanuman. Making an alliance with the quadrumana, he continued the pursuit until the enemy was overtaken in his own city, which was conquered and burned, the demon slain, and the lovely bride restored to her victorious husband, who carried her back to his recovered kingdom and throne.[1]

This incarnation is one of the most popular among the many objects of Vishnu worship. The mere utterance of the name of Rama is equal in religious merit to the giving of a hundred ornamented cows to a Brahman, or the performance of an Ashva-medha, besides being much cheaper than either.

A follower of Rama enjoys happiness in this world, and in the next is absorbed into Rama in the heaven of Vishnu. His devotees will still sit for days and nights together, upon the bank of the sacred Ganges, or beneath the stately pipal trees, repeating in low monotonous tones: "Ram, Ram, Rama." The mere utterance of the words, without any conception of their meaning, will secure a birth into a higher life, and if a bird or an animal should be so fortunate as to overhear the tones, they too will speedily be born into a more joyful state of existence.

Every year the Ramlila festival, held in many

[1] Reed's *Hindu Literature* pp. 153–271

places, commemorates Rama's adventures. The great poem has been set to music and is sung with much enthusiasm. In Benares the Maharaja celebrates the annual festival with great pomp. In Delhi, more than eighty-five thousand people according to native authorities accompany the procession as it passes through the principal bazars at night.

*Bala-Rama*. It is claimed by followers of Krishna that this older brother is an incarnation of the thousand-headed serpent Shesha who supports the earth upon his numerous heads, and earthquakes are caused by the movement of some one of them. He is sometimes called the Indian Hercules because he wields a ponderous club besides a ploughshare. The two brothers belonged to the tribe of Yadavas, who were cowherds and made their living from cattle by driving them from one locality to another, selling milk, butter, and curds. While they were yet children, their tribe came near a grove of palm trees where lived a terrible demon by the name of Dehunuka.

The lads were attracted by the sight of ripe fruit on the trees and wandered near the spot where the demon was feasting on the flesh of a deer, but all unconscious of his presence they shook the tree and brought down some fruit. Hearing the noise the malignant fiend left his feast, and assuming the form of a wild ass, he rushed upon the intruders and gave the older boy a terrific kick in the breast; undaunted by the blow, however, the powerful Bala-Rama seized his foe by the heels, and swung him around until he was dead, then tossed him into the top of a large palm tree, thus shaking off great quantities of fruit.

The other demons in the grove assumed the same form and rushed upon the boys, to avenge the death of their leader. But Bala-Rama with the help of Krishna treated them all in the same way, and when they were through, the trees were laden with wild asses and the ground was covered with fruit on which the cowherds feasted for many a day.[1]

*Krishna Vasudeva.* The son of Vasudeva who was the eighth child of the wife Devaki is the famous deity who was finally given a place as the eighth incarnation of Vishnu, although he belongs to a later period than the early avatars; the Hindus themselves claim that he appeared in the end of the third age of the world. The name means "black," or "dark coloured," and is so common in

[1] Vishnu-purana, Wilson's Trans., p. 517. The story is told in much the same way in some of the other Puranas.

India that it would appear to be given to every child who is unusually dark.

The earliest mention of the name is in the Rig-veda, where Indra is praised for having slain the wives of one Krishna; afterward the same god is said to have killed fifty thousand Krishnas, all of whom were black demons. There is also an early legend to the effect that a demon named Krishna, the black, advanced with ten thousand of his followers to the banks of the Ansumati River, where he (or they) committed fearful depredations, until he was defeated by Indra and stripped of his black skin.

In the Maha-bharata the name is given to a woman, but in this case there is a diacritical point on the final letter, which gives it the feminine form. It is then applied to the Princess Draupadi, who married five brothers, becoming the wife of each of them the same day.

Some details of a Krishna are found in the Maha-bharata, but they do not belong to the plot and have the appearance of being interpolations. The Krishna here mentioned is not the hero of the epic but appears as a chieftain who takes the part of the real heroes, and in more than one instance he advises dishonourable warfare. Krishna appears as a god in the Bhagavad-gita, a long philosophical discourse which is now found in the Maha-bharata, but the consensus of opinion among Oriental scholars is to the effect that it really belongs to a more modern period. It is to the Puranas of the Middle Ages that we have to look for the details of the life of this deity, and the stories are there given with great fulness of description and extravagant eulogy.

There, as elsewhere, he is said to be the eighth child of his mother, and the Vishnu-purana volunteers the further statement that the first six of these children were the offspring of a demon by the name of Hiranyakasipu.[1] His father, Vasudeva, was a cowherd, but not a chieftain of his tribe. It is claimed that the mission of Krishna was the destruction of Kansa, the tyrant king, who tried to forestall him by killing the babe; but he was saved by his father, who carried him away in the night and exchanged him for another child; the boy was therefore brought up by his foster parents, Nanda, and his wife, Yasoda.

Many of his childish exploits are given in the Puranas, and the pictures of the boy-thief stealing butter and curds and carrying off the garments of the bathers are still very attractive to his worshippers. He is represented as the hero of many

[1] Vishnu-purana, Wilson's trans., p. 498.

adventures; it is said that while he was still a youth, the cowherds were planning to offer an elaborate sacrifice to Indra, and Krishna dissuaded them from doing so. He claimed that they ought to pay their homage to the spirits of the mountains as they were in greater need of protection from them than from the god of storms. These spirits are hostile demons who wander whither they will, and if displeased with those who inhabit the forest, they assume the form of lions, and other beasts of prey, and kill the offenders. Therefore in obedience to Krishna, the cowherders worshipped the mountains, making offerings of curds, milk, and flesh.

Indra, being thus defrauded of his usual adulation, was very angry, and calling upon his cohorts of attending clouds, he gave orders for a fearful storm.

The clouds, obedient to his will, blended their powers, and in an instant the thunders pealed, the lightnings flashed, and the pitiless rain poured down, not only from above, but apparently from every side. Then Krishna plucked up a mountain, and held it aloft with one hand, calling upon his people to come under it. The herds of cattle, the waggons with goods were quickly driven under the great mountain umbrella, and there, also, the men, women, and children found shelter. Krishna received their adoration while for seven days and nights he still held it up.

At the end of this time, the storm king became weary, and commanded the elements to be at peace; then Krishna restored the mountain to its proper place. When the sunlight flooded the landscape, Indra himself praised Krishna, and by the direction of the grateful cows made him Govinda, or Prince of the Cattle, and this is the name he often bears.[1]

After this, the Gopis—the wives and daughters of the cowherds—strove with each other for the attentions of the god. It is said:

> They considered every instant without him as a myriad of years; and prohibited in vain by husbands, fathers, and brothers, they went forth at night to sport with Krishna, the object of their affections.

One evening while they were all dancing upon the green, the demon Arishto, disguised as a savage bull, rushed upon them. "His colour was like that of a dark cloud, his great horns were sharp and fearful; his eyes were like two fiery suns; as he moved, he ploughed up the ground with his hoofs." When he came bellowing toward them,

[1] Vish. Pur., pp. 522–28.

the Gopis cried to Govinda for help, and the youth stood like a statue waiting the approach of the foe. As soon as he was near enough, he caught him by the horns, and wrung his throat as if it had been a piece of wet cloth, then tearing off one of his horns, he beat the demon with it until he died.[1]

This story is told more in detail in the Harivansa. Afterward he killed another demon who attacked him in the form of a monstrous horse, but he thrust a powerful arm down the throat of his assailant until the great horse was choked to death.

*Wives of Krishna.* Many of his adventures are less creditable and the stories of his numerous wives occupy much space in the sacred books. It is said that "he came down from heaven to be the lover of Radha," but the other Gopis to the number of thousands were included in his attentions.

The second wife was Jambavati, the daughter of a bear. This marriage could only take place after a terrible contest with the grizzly father of the bride. Krishna fought the big bear for twenty-one consecutive days, and at last conquered him. The bear then exclaimed:

[1] Vish. Pur., pp. 535-36.

> Thou, mighty being, art surely invincible by all the demons and by the spirits of heaven, earth, and hell. Much less art thou to be vanquished by such as we, who are born of the brute creation.

Then humbly prostrating himself at the feet of the conqueror, he presented his daughter to Krishna as an offering suitable for a guest, and the bridegroom led the beautiful animal away in triumph.[1]

The third wife was the betrothed of another man, but the god carried the girl away by force, and afterward married her. Ruminiki appears to have been the next bride, but Krishna professed to be very tired of the marriage rites, and soon he married a great multitude of girls by the same ceremony.

The Purana says:

> Sixteen thousand and one hundred was the number of maidens (included in the last marriage), and into so many forms did he multiply himself that every one of the damsels thought he had wedded her in his single person, and the creator of the world—the assumer of universal shape—abode severally in the dwelling of each of these his wives.[2]

It is declared that these wives bore to Krishna one hundred and eighty thousand sons, and the

[1] Vish. Pur., p. 427. [2] *Ibid.*, p. 528.

Bhagavata-purana gives the names of about eighty of this numerous family.

*Death of the God.* In Dvaraka, the city of Krishna, according to the Purana, a hideous apparition representing death in a horrible form stalked in the streets and peered into the houses. Great consternation prevailed, and as its visits grew more frequent, the chief at last decided that the only remedy would be the destruction of the whole tribe.

Calling the Yadavas to gather at a sacred spot on the seashore, he besought them to render homage to a certain goddess, in the hope that she might avert the evils that seemed to threaten the city, and mayhap put an end to the visits of the ghastly spectre. They gathered at the coast in great numbers for this purpose—practically the whole tribe being in camp; but they brought with their supplies an abundance of wine, and soon the warriors were drinking freely, and quarrelling over their cups.

Then says the Purana:

Infuriated by the divine influence (of Krishna) they fell upon one another with missile weapons, and when these were expended, they had recourse to the rushes growing nigh. The rushes in their hands became as

> thunderbolts and with them they struck fatal blows. . . . Krishna, then, enraged, took up a handful of rushes to destroy them, and the rushes became a club of iron, and with this he slew many of the murderous Yadavas.[1]

After the members of the tribe, with his assistance, had fought to extermination, Krishna walked away with one surviving friend. They found his wounded brother Bala-Rama dying at the foot of a tree, and they waited until they saw his spirit come out of his mouth in the form of an enormous serpent and wend its way slowly to the seashore, where it soon disappeared in the waters.

Then Krishna gave his friend instructions to go to Dvaraka and carry the news of the death of his brother to Arjuna and others; he also charged him to inform their friends of his own approaching death. Then bidding his comrade farewell, he seated himself at the foot of a tree, sitting down Indian fashion with one foot supported upon the other knee:

> The illustrious Krishna sat engaged in thought resting his foot upon his knee. Then came a hunter named Jara . . . and beholding from a distance the foot of Krishna, he mistook it for a part of a deer, and shooting an arrow lodged it in the sole.[2] . . . Then

[1] Vish. Pur., p. 116.

[2] It is possible that we have here an echo of the vulnerable heel of Achilles.

the illustrious Krishna abandoned his mortal body, and the conditions of the threefold qualities; he became Nirguna—devoid of all qualities.

When Arjuna heard the news, he went with friends to the scene of the terrible mêlée where the murderous Yadavas had slain each other. And with the assistance of the Brahmans he gathered a great quantity of fuel and burned the bodies of the dead, not neglecting the proper funeral oblations. He then sent out searching parties to find the bodies of Krishna and Bala-Rama, and upon finding them, he carried them back to the city for the funeral rites to be performed there. When he approached the city he was distracted by the terrible howlings within her walls, for each of the sixteen thousand wives of the god seemed to think it was her wifely duty to make more outcry than any of the others.

We have graphic descriptions of this body of women with dishevelled hair, and loud voices filling the air with their wailings. Four of the widows were burned on his funeral pyre. Arjuna took the treasures of the city and the few survivors home with him, and settled them in Indra-prastha. Scarcely had they left the scene of much revelry and more crime, when the waves of the sea arose and swept the devoted city into her bosom. Fishes swam through the gilded halls of Dvaraka, and the sea mosses twined around her idols, while the moaning waves sang the requiem of fallen splendour and the billows chanted dirges for the dead.[1]

Although these things are not history in any true sense of that word, they at least represent their own side of the question—they give the oft-repeated assertions of their standard works on this subject.

[1] Vish. Pur., p. 116.

# CHAPTER VI

## PRESENT CONDITIONS (*Continued*)

Modern Krishna Worship. Hindu Gurus. The Gossains. European and American Fanatics.

VISHNU is adored under various names and in many localities. It is claimed that the constant repetition of a certain formula is of such efficiency that visions of the god are vouchsafed to those who are faithful in the performance of this duty.

One enthusiastic devotee who longed for this experience consulted a Brahman who, for a satisfactory reward, told him of the proper text, or mantra, which, if repeated for 800,000 times, would produce the desired result. This arduous task was accomplished by persevering in hard work nearly all the time, day and night, for three months. Then, as no vision followed, the victim went to the priest and told him of the failure of the experiment. The Brahman glibly explained, however, that some slight mistake must have been made in the utterance of some one word, and any such slip would necessitate the repetition of the whole performance until the task was completed without the slightest verbal slip, then the longed-for vision would come!

The most popular form of Vishnu, especially among the lower classes, is Krishna, and his images abound throughout the country. The mere mechanical repetition of one of his many names, even though the mind of the worshipper be fixed upon something else, secures admission into Vishnu's heaven. The worship of his images is very much like the daily homage paid to Shiva, the same process of dressing and undressing, washing, painting, and offering refreshments to the idol being constantly repeated in many localities, day after day, and year after year, for a lifetime—nay, for many lifetimes, for they are repeated from one generation to the next.

In Europe and America, however, we have as yet no large idols of Krishna to be painted, dressed, and adored, from morning until night, hence it has been necessary to somewhat modify the worship here.

A Krishna priest gives long and definite descriptions of the duties of the Vaishnava evidently intended for use on American and European soil. He says:

> The Krishna worshipper is either a householder or a hermit . . . the formula of worship and religious rule of life as practised by both the hermit and the householder are *practically the same.*

He then devotes hundreds of words to the definite rules concerning the invocations of the entire forenoon. Afterward he says:

> But this morning worship is not all that the householder Vaishnava performs to attain the love of Krishna. He eats or drinks nothing, without first offering it through some mystic formula to Krishna, and his food is pure vegetables, his drink pure water. In the evening he joins other Vaishnavas to tell of Krishna, hear of the sacred earthly acts of Krishna, sing of Krishna, and when the spirit of song moves him, he dances with others in ecstasy. *Besides these practices,* he repeats *many thousand times* the name of Krishna over his Tulsai rosary . . . a Vaishnava should, *at all times*, sing of Krishna.

Dr. Bhattacharya, the scholarly Brahman, devotes many pages to descriptions of some of the most loathsome Hindu sects and then says:

> With all his cleanliness, and vegetarianism, and teetotalism, the Vaishnava (or Krishna devotee) is perhaps the most dangerous in the whole list. . . . The moral laxity which he encourages by the stories of the illicit loves between his gods and goddesses, and by the strong tendency to imitate them which

his teachings generate, outweighs the good done by him.

Every man of common-sense naturally feels a horror at the Tantrik and the Aghori, but the Vaishnava insinuates himself in a manner that is irresistible. . . . The manner in which, in the case of Krishna, man-worship has degenerated into abomination worship may be traced step by step . . . the Bhagavata and Brahma Vaivarta throw aside every mask, and in the most shameless manner attempt to sanctify every form of debauchery, so as to enable the priestly class to gratify their lust. . . . The reader is called upon to admire and worship Krishna, on account of his having seduced the milkmaids of Brindavan by every kind of trick that the most wicked of human beings could invent.

The chief object of his love was one Radha, who, according to some of the authorities, was the wife of the brother of his foster-mother. The very name of this Radha is not now to be found even in the Bhag-vat. But by an abuse of scientific terms, she is represented by the latter-day Vishnuvites as the Prakriti, or the material basis of the Yoga philosophy, and Krishna is represented as the Purush by whose union with the Prakriti this universe was created.

In almost all the modern Vishnuvite shrines, an image of Radha is associated with that of Krishna, and in Northern India there are very few temples in which Ruminiki or any of the married wives of Krishna are worshipped with him.

The tales and songs connected with Radha and Krishna cannot for the sake of decency be referred to here. The reader, unacquainted with them, and curious to know their details, must take the trouble to read the two modern Puranas mentioned above, and also the work of Jaya-deva, Vidyapati, etc.

According to the legends contained in these works, when Krishna, by killing Kansa, became the virtual ruler of Mathura, he forsook not only Radha, and the other cowherd women of Brindavan, whom he had seduced, but, in the most heartless manner, disowned even his foster-parents.

These stories form the theme of the most heart-rending songs and odes, and being much more intelligible to all classes of women, both young and old, than the wars and intrigues of the Mahabharata, are much better calculated than anything else to enable the priest to acquire a hold on their hearts by awakening their tenderest sentiments.[1]

*Modern Hindu Gurus.* The Guru is a modern money-making invention who is not mentioned in the earlier literature of India. The word originally meant a teacher of the Vedas, and as such it conveyed the idea of respectability, but the Vedic mantras are too voluminous, and prosaic, to attract many pupils, and women are not allowed to study them at all, neither are the lower castes, hence pupils in these classes were so few in number that the income from them was exceedingly small.

The Tantriks, however, were equal to the

[1] Bhatt., *Hindu Castes and Sects*, pp. 391, 394, 431, 433.

emergency of furnishing profitable employment for any Brahman who could read, in this way: They gave the name of mantra to some mystic and meaningless syllables, which might be given to the pupil, and taught at a single sitting. The lowest castes, and even women, were made eligible to these classes, and almost any Brahman was enabled to collect around him an army of *chellas* who were bound by their vows to worship him as their god, and to pay a yearly tax to him and his descendants from generation to generation. In this vow the victim swears that: "*My soul, mind and body, are irrevocably sold to my Guru*," whose name is given, and then the ownership of his victim becomes absolute. When the sons of a deceased Guru make a division of his property, the *chellas* are counted as so many slaves, and are distributed among the heirs in the same way as the other properties belonging to the estate.

This simple method of inventing and installing Gurus in modern times is remarkably easy and successful. It is true that such mystic syllables as *hoong*, *doong*, *kling*, or *hring*, are, as Bhattacharya says,

> an outrage upon common-sense. But, [he adds], the gullibility of man has no limit, and the Guru who whispers these meaningless expressions into the

ears of his disciple is worshipped and paid by him (or her) as the bestower of untold benefits.

The *chella* is not allowed to reveal these mystic syllables to any one. The matter is certainly not such as to be capable of bearing the light of intelligent criticism. The Guru therefore acts wisely in insisting that the communication should be treated as strictly confidential. . . . Furthermore, those meaningless syllables, or short sentences, must be repeated by the *chella*, many times a day, and thus he is kept in constant bondage to the man who first whispered them into his or her ears.[1]

The Gurus are ingenious, also, about adding to their income in various ways. For instance, Ram Sarana Pal, belonging among the Gurus of Bengal, was a man of great originality. He proclaimed himself the proprietor of every human body, and claimed that he was entitled to rent from every human being for allowing his soul to occupy his body! In order to enforce this right, and to give a pecuniary interest to the most influential of his followers so as to strengthen his position with them, he appointed several of the chief men among them as agents and bailiffs, for collecting his revenue.

The majority of the dupes are women who gladly pay the small tax demanded of them for the

[1] Bhatt., pp. 27–28.

rental of the bodies of their husbands and children, so as to insure long life to their families.

Each agent of the Guru is generally on very friendly terms with some woman in the village, or group of villages, assigned to his care, and through the instrumentality of this woman, he is enabled to hold secret meetings which are attended by all the female votaries within his jurisdiction, and in which he plays the part of Krishna. The agents of the Guru are required to pay over to him all of their collections, except their own commissions, at a grand levee which is held by him at his family residence in the month of March.

At this time, the Guru performs the most wonderful miracles, curing leprosy, blindness, deafness, and other things which are beyond the reach of Hindu medication. A Brahman, writing from near the scene of action, describes one "cure" as follows:

> The crowd was great, but the blind man managed to elbow his way through it and bring his case to the notice of the Guru. . . . Suddenly he was seized by attendants and taken to a near-by tank, where sand was vigorously rubbed into his eyes while he cried out in agony. . . . While they were doing it they kept asking whether his sight was restored or not. . . . Finding there was no other escape from the torture he

at last said it was, and then a great shout went up that a marvellous cure had been effected.

"He was made to bathe in the tank, for washing away the sand, and then he was carried in triumph through the crowd, being borne aloft in the air, like a Roman victor. After this advertisement of the miracle, the victim was deported from the village so secretly that it was impossible for any of the pilgrims to ascertain the truth of the matter, and it is very likely that one of the attendants represented himself as the blind man who had been restored to his sight.

Guru worship is naturally favoured by the priest-ridden Hindu everywhere, but it is only among certain classes that a god would be humiliated for the honour of this man. The drinking of such water as has been used for washing the feet of the Guru is common enough, but some of his devotees will go much farther in their adoration.

The Gurus are mostly of two classes, the Tantrik and the Vaishnava. The Tantriks inculcate and enforce the homage to the wives of Shiva, and the worship of courtesans. They also claim that while meeting together for the practice of the Bacchanalian rites, all the members of their orgies have a higher position than that of the most exalted Brahmans.

The Vaishnavas enforce the equally degrading

worship of either Krishna, or some other incarnation of Vishnu, which often includes the Guru or the Gossain. Both sects agree that the Gurus are a necessity, and that they must be well paid by those who have sold themselves, "*body, soul, and mind*," into this abject slavery.

*The Gossains.* This word is a corruption of Goswami, which is a compound consisting of *go* and *swami*. *Swami* means an owner,—a lord or master,—hence when it is assumed by a Frenchwoman it is at least a misnomer.[1] *Go* has several meanings, such as cow, earth, mountain, etc. Hence the word Goswami may mean "Lord of Cows," "Lord of Mountains," "Owner of the Earth," etc. "Lord of the Cows" is one of the favourite titles of Krishna and at present his worshippers are divided into several sects—indeed the greater part of modern Hinduism is apparently divided between the idolatry connected with Shiva and his wives, and the followers of Krishna, and the devotion paid to his female favourites, which follows along the same corrupt lines.

The ex-Chief Justice of Indore, in his address

[1] Dr. Chas. R. Lanman, Professor of Sanskrit at Harvard University, in a recent letter to the author says: "Don't fail to point out that the Swamis are self-appointed '*Lords*' or '*Owners.*' 'Svamin' means 'owner' from *svam*, 'own.'"

before the Congress of Orientalists held in London, well says that:

One of the most remarkable features of Krishna worship is the blind homage paid to the Gossains of the Vallabh sect.

The cult is of recent origin, and its principal doctrine is that of faith, or Bhakti—of sacrificing everything for the Guru. Their mantras for the common people are, "*Sri Krishna Sarakam mam*" (My shelter is Krishna), or "*Kling Krishnaya; Gopi Jan ballabhaya Swaha*" (Swaha to Krishna, the beloved of the Gopis).

For the richer and more well-to-do, the mantra is longer. Translated into English it is: "Sri Krishna is my refuge from the sorrows and troubles caused by separation of hundreds of years, and from unlimited time; for the removal of these, *I offer to Lord Krishna my body, its organs, their functions, wife (or husband), house, son, wealth, and all that I have.* I am thy slave, Krishna."

The Gossains of this sect represent themselves to be so many embodiments of Krishna, and expect and receive from their followers, not only a dedication of their wealth and money, but of their persons, especially the female and handsomer portion of them.[1]

Some parts of this worship would appear to the outsider to be innocent enough, but its inevitable tendency, especially where it is joined with recitations from the poem of Jaya-deva, the Bhagavata-purana, and other works of that class, is

[1] Ex-Chief Justice, *Trans. Ninth Internat. Cong.*, vol. i., p. 145.

to develop all the immoralities of the Krishna and Radha ceremonies.

Serious charges of this nature were brought against the Gossains in the celebrated case of the Bombay Maharajas which came before the Supreme Court of Bombay, and in the judgment rendered by Sir Matthew Sausse he says:

> All songs connected with the god Krishna, which were brought before us, were of an amorous character, and it appeared that songs of a corrupting and licentious tendency, both in ideas and expressions, are sung by young females to the Maharaja (or Gossain) upon festive occasions in which they are identified with the god in his most licentious aspect.[1]

The testimony given by Judge Lala Baijnath refers to the times since the criminal practices of the priests were considerably checked by the results of this celebrated trial.

But still in the temples where the priests do homage to the idols, men and women perform their acts of adoration to the Gossains. One mode of worshipping the idols is swinging them, and the women worship, not the god, but the priest or Gossain by swinging him in a pendant seat. The work of swinging the idol would be far easier, but that has already been done by the Maharaja,

[1] Sausse, *History of the Bombay Maharajas*, p. 142.

who now takes his ease in the swinging seat at the expense of his tired devotees, who do the work, and also pay well for the privilege of doing it!

Not only this, but the *pan-supra*, or saliva ejected from his mouth, the leavings of his food, and the very dust whereon he has walked, are eagerly eaten by them. The water in which the dirty images have been washed is "holy water," and the devotees also eagerly drink that in which the garments of the Gossains have been washed, while that in which their feet have been bathed is called *Caran-amrita*, or "feet nectar," and it is used in the same way.

In an address delivered before an English audience, and reported by the *London Daily News* Narayan Seshadri boasted that he himself had claimed and received divine honours, and had seen believers among his own countrymen greedily drink the water in which his feet had been washed.

> But infinitely worse than all this—it is believed that the best mode of propitiating them [the Gossains] is by ministering to their sensual appetites. Body, soul, and property (*tan*, *man*, *dhan*) must be wholly made over to them, by their disciples, and their women are taught to believe that the highest bliss will be secured to themselves and their families by the caresses of Krishna's representatives."[1]

[1] Williams, *Hind.*, p. 145.

Like the Hindu priests in Europe and America, the Gossains are thrifty souls, and they demand good prices for whatever honours they may condescend to bestow upon their devotees. In a work written by a Brahman and published in Calcutta, we find the prices of these favours well defined. He says:

Their tariff is as given below:
For homage by sight, five rupees.[1]

For homage by touch, twenty rupees.

For the honour of washing the Maharaja's foot, thirty-five rupees.

For swinging him, forty rupees.

For rubbing sweet unguents on his body, forty-two rupees.

For being allowed to sit with him on the same couch, sixty rupees.

For being closeted with him in the same room, from fifty to five hundred rupees.

For eating *pan* (spittle) from the mouth of the Maharaja, seventeen rupees.

For the privilege of dancing with him, from one hundred to two hundred rupees.

For drinking the water in which he has bathed, seventeen rupees.[2]

[1] A rupee is about forty-eight cents.

[2] Bhatt., *H. C. and S.*, p. 457.

If such prices as these are exacted from the poor people of India for these honours, we can only imagine what rates are paid by rich white women who follow after the same notorious characters.

*European and American Fanatics.* One would hardly expect to find this confessedly corrupt cult flourishing in the United States, but a book recently written by a Krishna priest and published on American soil is dedicated: "*To my Guru, to whom my Soul, Mind, and Body are irrevocably sold, in payment of the grace of his illumination which lighted my path to the Lotus feet of Krishna, my Beloved.*"

Hence we can easily see the character of the vows which must *finally* be taken by this man's devotees, and cease to wonder that so many of them find at last a refuge,—not in Krishna, but in the asylums.

And yet, knowing these things, the Swamis are constantly advocating Krishnaism on both European and American soil. They know their own official works are the exponents of the character of the boy thief, the dishonourable warrior, the licentious lover, and all of the unspeakable obscenity connected even with his *public* worship, in places where they dare go through with the whole ceremony, and they know that this idolatry is utterly degrading to all who are tainted therewith, and yet they are persistently teaching it in such language as the following:

> Krishna is Love itself, the Love that draws the Lover and the Loved closest to each other. *It knows no ceremony*, knows no formal respect. It knows no motive. *Love is its own cause, motive, and satisfaction. It knows no barrier*, sees no faults, nay sees *virtue* in *faults*.

A Chicago woman who entertained one of the Hindu priests in her home said she had "never heard any one talk so beautifully about L-o-v-e"!

Family ties are not allowed to intervene in any way between the Swamis and their devotees, for the official statement is:

> It knows no barrier! We know thee, O Krishna [or thy representatives,] as one greater and nearer to us than our husbands, brothers, and fathers; and even at the risk of their displeasure to us, we come to lay at thy feet our poor offerings and our hearts.

It was in harmony with this creed that the wife of a prominent educator abandoned her family, with the announcement: "My husband and children are no more to me than others who are equally deserving of my regard. My religion teaches me that they have no claim on me!"

In one of our great cities, the headquarters of a Hindu cult are, or were until very recently, in charge of an American woman who had taken the terrible vows, and the veil of an Indian nun. Her associates declared: "We know nothing of former relationships. She now belongs more to us than to her family!"

A well-known New England woman, having fallen under the hypnotic sway of a Swami, made over her entire fortune at his dictation. After the papers were safely made out, the "further mysteries" were revealed to her. Can we wonder that she then went hopelessly insane and was for years—in the asylum?

The Gurus do not, *as yet*, bring their most hideous idols with them—only some little image before which to say one's prayers "so as to aid in concentration." But far worse than idolatry before images is the man-worship which they inculcate and enforce,—the slavish devotion to the priests.

One well-known Swami was in the habit of receiving the adoration of his followers, when he came out of his "daily meditation. Then these American women were ready to caress his robe, and kiss his sandaled feet!

It sometimes happens that a Swami or Guru

takes a foreign trip from the Middle West, by way of New York, when the most palatial ocean steamer and the most luxurious Pullman cars are allowed to carry him abroad and through the principal cities of Europe. On these occasions he sometimes tolerates the companionship of the rich woman who pays all the bills!

"He was my man-god" (or Guru), wailed the poor New York girl over the body of the creature she worshipped, and tried to follow into the land of shadows, by way of suicide!

To the "holy men" it surely is a wonderful change from their native poverty, to Western wealth and luxury. Squatting in a loin-cloth at the gate of a heathen temple, as many of them do, and receiving alms from the passers-by, is not nearly so attractive as sitting in luxuriously furnished parlours, while their dupes bring in their delicate or valuable offerings.

Money and costly presents given to their "man-god" counts greatly to the "accumulated merit" of European and American women, but while they receive a vast amount of lip flattery from the objects of their devotion, they are inwardly held in contempt, for no woman can cheapen herself, without paying the terrible penalty. What wonder that Vivekananda, on his return to his native soil, spread the report that American women were, in character, even like the dancing girls of India?

There are too many even in civilised countries, who are entranced with doctrines which are *claimed* to represent Krishnaism, but the philosophy which is at first presented for their approval is only the beginning of the unspeakable worship pertaining to "the dark god."

The final vows are a horrible secret which cannot be revealed under penalty of punishments which are far worse than death—it would at last bring upon the devoted heads of the victims the curses of all the gods in the Hindu pantheon!

A poor desolated and deserted girl in New York at last testified that a vein was opened in her arm, and she was compelled to sign her vows with a pen dipped in her own blood!

Let the white woman beware of the hypnotic influence of the East—let her remember that when her Guru, or god-man, has once whispered his mystic syllables into her ear[1] and she has sworn allegiance to him, she is for ever helpless in his hands.

The Swami, Gossain, or Guru is now quite at home in both Europe and America and many a desolated home lies in the trail of his silken robes.

[1] See p. 118.

When for any reason they are forced out of one community, other cities, other aliases, and other victims are always waiting for them farther on. For instance one of the most popular Swamis in the Eastern States left Chicago, according to the newspapers, at the strenuous invitation of an indignant husband. Another, who is now doing a flourishing business in California, left the same city on account of irreconcilable difficulties with the police.

Certain it is, that if our clean-hearted American women were acquainted with the true character of the cult, they would flee its contaminating influence. But "the further mysteries" are not revealed until the victim is beyond the reach of any returning mental health, and the descent to heathenism has been so gradual, and the way has been painted in such alluring colours, that she has been unconscious of her destination until it was too late.

Let our people read the standard Hindu works on this subject,—let them look into the pages of the Vishnu-purana, which may be found in English translation in our large libraries, let them study the Bhagavata-purana; they are both devoted to the glorification of Krishna, and they both show him to be the worst type of a shameless sensualist, faithless lover, and undutiful son. Lacking these, let them read the works of English scholars like Sir Monier Monier-Williams or Prof. F. Max Müller. If they will only investigate the matter in any sane and scholarly way, all illusions on this subject will quickly vanish, and the priests of Hinduism will no longer be able to "creep into houses and lead captive silly women."

# CHAPTER VII

## IMITATIONS OF OLD TESTAMENT HISTORY

The Work of Translators. Imposition upon Wilford. Teachers of Hinduism. Adam and Eve. Story of the Flood. Abraham and Isaac. The Gita-govinda.

THE literature of India is colossal in its proportions, and it was not until the 19th century that its problems were solved by English-speaking scholars. This was necessarily done by a division of labour, for life is too short to enable any one worker to obtain from original sources a complete knowledge of Indian philology, language, and history.

That prince of philologists, Prof. F. Max Müller, devoted twenty of the best years of his life to the Rig-veda alone. Colonel Colin Mackenzie spent many years in collecting and arranging thirty-four large folio volumes of manuscripts, but his careful methods were of inestimable value to those who came after him.

A thorough study of the Puranas alone would occupy half a century, but a year devoted to the excellent translations of the late Horace Hayman Wilson will give one a very good idea of their contents.

The Hindus themselves claim, in the Padmapurana, that these books "consisted originally of one thousand million stanzas, but four hundred thousand of them were thought to be sufficient for the instruction of men, and the rest were preserved for the gods."

These "four hundred thousand stanzas," however, are equal to sixteen hundred thousand lines, and the student has reason to be thankful that the gods kept the greater portion of these books for their own private use!

The literature of India was never properly classified—it was never published, even in the Sanskrit tongue, until it was done by European scholars, under the auspices of England's greatest university.

The fact that these books had for centuries been transmitted from one generation to the next only by constant repetition and memorising by the students gave them a weird influence over the Anglo-Saxon as well as over the Asiatic. And when we remember that the Veda among the Hindus occupies very much the position accorded to the Old Testament in Hebrew letters—that it is as sacred to the Indian as our Scriptures are to us—we cannot wonder that it has attracted the attention of scholars in every part of the world.

*Imposition upon Wilford.* According to Max Müller, the pandits were greatly opposed to the translation of the Veda from the Sanskrit. They were obliged to admit that the edition was complete and authentic, but it took from them their principal weapon against the missionaries.

"In former times, they had been accustomed to declare that there was no commandment in the Old Testament, no precept in the New, which had not been anticipated in the Vedas, and when the incredulous missionary asked for the manuscript, he was coolly informed that so sacred a document must not be touched by an unbeliever!"[1] It was also asserted that "the sacred books of the Hindus were thousands of years older than the Old Testament, which had indeed been largely borrowed from them!"

Men who should have been more careful allowed these statements in some cases to pass unchallenged, while eager sceptics hailed the idea with delight, and added very largely to the stories thus set afloat.

Men and women, too, who could not tell to save

[1] Max Müller, *Chips*, vol. ii., p. 304.

their lives what a Veda might be, were very loud and confident in their assertions that the whole Bible had been borrowed from books whose names they could not spell, nor pronounce after they had been spelled!

It was under these circumstances that Lieut. Wilford took up the work of investigation in Calcutta. He had become convinced that the Hindus possessed in their literature some of the myths found in Greek and Roman mythology, and not only this, but he had an idea that the narratives of the Old Testament had possibly been derived from the same source, and he determined to verify the supposition.

With this object in view, he cultivated the friendship of the priests, finding their affections were easily won by gifts which were more or less costly, and then availed himself of this acquaintance for the examination of the problems involved. He then told them the principal stories of classical mythology and the leading events in Old Testament history; he assured them they would find these things in their own sacred books, if they would only look for them, but no results were forthcoming. He then held out hopes of goodly financial rewards if they would find them, and this offer worked like magic.

Soon they placed in his hands manuscripts containing the very things he sought, and for these the priests received generous compensation. The stories of Deukalion and Prometheus—of Adam and Eve—of Abraham and Sarah followed each other in quick succession.

The demand created a large supply and for several years one essay after another appeared in the volumes of the *Asiatic Researches*. There were myths of classical mythology, and narratives closely resembling the stories of the Old Testament, all of which "had been translated from the ancient books of India"!

Surprise and excitement prevailed in scholarly circles over these discoveries. There was great excitement, not only in Calcutta, but also in London, Paris, and the German universities.

The Sanskrit manuscripts which Wilford had obtained were submitted to Sir William Jones and others who were considered the best Sanskrit scholars of their day, and they pronounced them genuine; it is true that many wise men remained incredulous, but there were the manuscripts to show for themselves, and the work went merrily on.

At last, however, the supply corresponded so exactly with the amount of money furnished that the documents were again, and more carefully, examined. It was then found that clever forgeries had been committed—that pages which had been aged by a peculiar process had been inserted in manuscripts which were undoubtedly old, and on them the wily priests had written the classical and biblical stories which they had learned from the lips of the enthusiastic officer.

Wilford, who by this time had become a Colonel, did not hesitate to admit that he had been victimised. He made a manly confession which was a warning to others, and Sir William Jones openly admitted that he also had been deceived, but during the infancy of Sanskrit studies it had been easy to perpetrate this gigantic fraud upon students of limited experience.

Says Max Müller:

> It is perfectly true that at the present time, after the progress which has been made in accurate and critical study of the Sanskrit, it would be unpardonable if any scholar accepted as genuine, such passages as were translated by Sir William Jones, yet it is by no means certain that a further study may not lead to similar disenchantments and deprive many a book in Sanskrit literature of its high claims to antiquity . . . and those who have believed in their extreme antiquity will then be held up to ridicule like Sir William Jones and Lieutenant Wilford.[1]

[1] Max Müller, *Chips*, vol. v., p. 109.

*Teachers of Hinduism.* The essays which had been so ignorantly constructed upon a false basis were widely read, and are still quoted by people who have never heard of Wilford's confession, or if they have heard, they choose to ignore it. Not only this but rumours grow as they spread, and we have many Americans as well as Europeans who are quick to catch at anything and everything which seems to bring discredit upon the Scriptures.

It is also true that Hinduism as taught in Europe and America is very different from the genuine article. These "missionaries from the Orient," who are teaching the milder forms, and even misrepresentations of their own sacred books, are very careful to keep out of the sight of beginners those doctrines and ceremonies which would at once repel clean-hearted Anglo-Saxons.

They present vague, illusive, and often attractive theories without offering any definite form of proof, and indeed the class of people who are delighted with any new fad do not need any historical evidence. For instance a Hindu, who was evidently a Buddhist, in conversation with a Chicago lady discoursed eloquently upon the marvellous phenomena produced by the Mahatmas in the mountains of Thibet and elsewhere.

At last she enquired: "How may I know positively that such beings exist?"

Said he: "Do you not sometimes have ideas, and do not know where they come from?"

"Yes," she quickly answered.

"That is it—there is the proof for which you ask—*they come* from the Mahatmas!"

The pathetic feature of the incident is found in the fact that she seemed to be entirely satisfied with the proof (?) thus obtained. And hence, because so few people are willing to investigate these things in a reasonable way, these teachers are reaping a harvest of English, French, and American money while claiming that even the Puranas "were written thousands and thousands of years ago"!

There are foolish women in some of our large cities who are actually forcing their indulgent husbands into financial ruin, by squandering their money in secret, upon these wily adventurers. It is often done without the husband's knowledge, and confession is sometimes made to a friend that the demands are constantly growing larger, and the victim cannot see any way of escape. But the work goes wickedly on.

One of these "teachers" very truthfully remarked: "We find America a better place than

India in which to teach Krishnaism"! There is no valid excuse for being thus victimised, when our libraries contain the works of standard authors on this subject, but some of the admirers of the cult have actually rushed into print with assertions that make them the laughing stock of scholars.

Even if the doctrines of Hinduism were absolutely true, they never could be of the slightest benefit to either Europeans or Americans, who cannot by any amount of penance purchase admission at death to either of the heavens—they cannot become worthy of recognition by these people except in a financial way. The sole benefit which they can derive is the privilege of admiring those who sneer at them in secret, and then continue to pour their money into the pockets which are constantly crying for more.

In vain may Europeans go to India, assume Indian aliases, and return claiming to be "swamis"; they must always be known as impostors, not only by a genuine swami, but by every one who is at all acquainted with the subject.

Sir Monier Monier-Williams says:

> The truth certainly is that no stranger can be admitted as a convert to Hinduism, either by making any particular confession of faith, or by going through any prescribed forms. *The only acknowledged mode*

*of admission is by birth.* To become a Hindu, one must be born a Hindu.[1]

And yet, inducements are held out which are contrary to the fundamental principles of the Hindu religions. Our land is flooded with literature which is well calculated to deceive the careless and thoughtless—it is flooded with reckless assertions on this subject which are repeated over and over again from the platform, many of the speakers blindly following each other, without making any effort to find out for themselves whether or not there is a particle of truth in what they are saying. They are issued in book form, in pamphlet form, they are being sent out through the medium of the newspapers wherever they can find admission to these columns, and they are going through the mails in the form of private correspondence, France, England, Germany, and Russia being especially unfortunate in Europe, while our own land is also receiving the especial attention of numerous invaders.

*Adam and Eve.* The acme of literary dishonesty is attained when so-called "quotations" are deliberately *manufactured* in order to suit a certain

[1] Williams, *Brahmanism and Hinduism*, p. 98.

theory, and this sort of work has been done in numberless instances.

We now have stories written up in imitation of Old Testament narratives and we are unblushingly told that these things "are from the Veda"!

Extracts from a parody on Adam and Eve run as follows:

> Having created the man and woman and animated them with the divine afflatus—the Lord said unto them: "Behold your mission is to the people of this beautiful island [Ceylon] where I have gathered together everything pleasant, and needful for your subsistence." . . .
>
> And thus saying, the Lord disappeared . . . then Adima and Heva dwelt together in perfect happiness: but ere long a vague disquietude began to creep upon them. . . . The spirit of evil, jealous of their felicity and of the work of Brahma, inspired them with disturbing thoughts. "Let us wander through the island," said Adima to his companion, "and see if we may not find some part of it more beautiful than this." . . .
>
> And Heva followed her husband . . . wandering for days and months. But as they advanced, the woman was seized with strange terrors. "Adima," said she, "let us go no farther. It seems to me that we are disobeying the Lord; have we not already quitted the place he assigned us for a dwelling and forbade us to leave?"
>
> "Fear not," said Adima, "this is not the fearful wilderness of which he spake unto us."
>
> And they wandered on . . . arriving at last at the

extremity of the island, the two wanderers stood amazed; the country before them was covered with stately trees, birds of a thousand colours flitted midst their foliage.

"Behold what beautiful things," cried Adima, "and what good fruit such trees must produce! Let us go and taste them, and if that country is better than this, we will dwell there."

Heva, trembling, besought Adima to do nothing which might irritate the Lord against them.

"Are we not well here? Wherefore seek other things?"

"True," replied Adima, "but we will come back; what harm can it be to have visited this unknown country that presents itself to our view?"

Then placing his wife upon his shoulders, he proceeded to cross the space that separated him from the object of his desires.

But no sooner did they touch the shore than trees, flowers, birds, all they had seen from the opposite side vanished midst terrific clamour; the rocks by which they had crossed sunk into the waters, a few sharp peaks alone remaining above the surface. . . . Adima threw himself weeping upon the sands . . . but Heva, throwing herself into his arms, besought him not to despair. . . . "Let us rather pray to the Author of all good to pardon us."

The above is a bit of modern fiction from which it is asserted the story of Adam and Eve was borrowed; it has been ingeniously prepared, with variations enough to give colour to the charge of plagiarism, but nothing of the sort can be found in the genuine books of India, from one end to the other!

Other parodies have been perpetrated with the cool announcement that "these things are found in the Bhagavad-gita" only the word is wrongly spelled by the impostor, who had probably never seen the book!

Poor France, especially, has been flooded with this sort of literature, while England and America have by no means escaped.

Max Müller says of these base forgeries and the book which contains them:

> Many of the words which J—— quotes as Sanskrit, are not Sanskrit at all; others never have the meaning which he assigns to them; and as to the passages [claimed to be] from the Veda, including the Bhagavad-gita, *they are not from the Veda,* they are not from any old Sanskrit writer—they simply belong to the latter half of the nineteenth century.[1]

*Story of the Flood.* The survivors of the great deluge evidently handed down to their posterity an account of the leading events connected therewith, and hence nearly every people on the globe have their tradition concerning it. The same voice comes to us from the archives of Babylon, from

[1] Max Müller, *Chips*, vol. v., p. 128.

the clay tablets of Assyria, from the parchments of China, from the manuscripts of India, from the annals of Greece, and more recently from the temple library found in the ruins of Nippur.

Amidst so many independent witnesses it is not necessary to conclude that any of them are borrowed from each other; like some of the others, however, the Hindu tradition is so buried in mythology that without other evidence on the subject one would never conclude that it was based on historic fact.

And yet, a Hindu priest, writing on American soil, unblushingly asserts: "The account of the deluge as given in the Old Testament has been taken from minute accounts recorded in the Matsya Purana and the condensed facts about them given in all the Puranas."

That is, the biblical story of the flood as recorded in the Book of Genesis—one of the oldest books of the Old Testament—"was taken from the Puranas," which were written during the Middle Ages of the Christian era!

He never would make such an absurdly false statement as this, if he did not know that he could place the most implicit confidence, in the utter ignorance of his devotees!

*Abraham and Isaac.* One of the manufactured quotations above alluded to is founded upon this narrative in Genesis, and we are gravely told that: "This is the original from which the story of Abraham and Isaac was taken."

In this case, they have come nearer to the truth than is their wont, from the fact that there is found in the Aitareya-brahmana a legend concerning the offering of a son.

But this Brahmana belongs to a period more than a thousand years this side of Abraham, and not only this, but the difference in the stories is so radical and far reaching that the idea of plagiarism on either side must be ignored by the careful critic.

The legend of Sunahsepa has been well translated by more than one scholar, and runs about as follows:

King Harischandra had no son; therefore he went to the great sage, Narada, and enquired, "What benefit comes from a son?" Narada replied:

> A father, by his son clears off a debt,
> In him, a self is born of self. The pleasure
> A father has in his son exceeds
> All other pleasures. Food is life, apparel
> Is protection, gold an ornament;
> A loving wife the best of friends, a daughter

An object of compassion, but a son
Is like a light sent from highest heaven.

Go then to Varuna, the god, and say—
'Let but a son be born, O King, to me
And I will sacrifice that son to thee!'

An Indian is always in debt to his forefathers until he has a son of his own, because the happiness of the dead depends upon certain ceremonies which can be performed only by a son. Those who have lived in India or have read authoritative works on the subject will understand why "a daughter is an object of compassion."

According to the instructions of the sage, the king went to Varuna, and made his plea and promise.

In due time a son was born who was named Rohita, but time passed on and still the king did not fulfil his vow, and at last the angry god afflicted him with dropsy as a penalty for the long delay.

The lad had now attained to years of some understanding, and the royal father explained to him the conditions of his birth and told him that he must prepare for sacrifice.

Not liking the prospect before him, the boy took his bow and arrows and fled into the forest. For six long years, he roamed through the wilderness, living upon the wild fruits and what game he could secure, but still the sentence of death was hanging over him.

At last he found a hermit who was a Brahman, but he was living in the wilderness with his wife and three sons, and Rohita entered into negotiations with the father to procure a substitute. The hermit agreed to sell one of his sons for the sacrifice if the prince would give him a hundred cows! A bargain was quickly made, and Rohita set off for home with the boy, Sunahsepa, by his side. In order to witness the horrible rite, the unnatural father went also.

Taking the victim to the king, the prince explained:

> "Father, this boy shall be my substitute."
> Then Harischandra went to Varuna
> And prayed: "Accept this ransom for my son."
> The god replied: "Let him be sacrificed,
> A Brahman is more worthy than a king."

The preparations were made, and the intended victim was led forth.

Four great Rishis, or sages, officiated as priests, but they could find no one who would consent to bind the beautiful child who was to be offered. In this extremity the barbaric parent again came to the rescue, and for the sake of adding to his large herd of cattle, he volunteered to bind his boy upon the sacrificial altar.

> "Give me a hundred cows and I will bind him."
> They gave them to him and he bound the boy.
> But now, no person would consent to kill him.
> Then said the father, "Give me yet again
> Another hundred cows, and I will slay him!"
>
> Once more they gave the hundred, and the father
> Whetted his knife to sacrifice his son;
> Then said the child: "Let me implore the gods,
> Haply they may deliver me from death."
>
> So Sunahsepa prayed to all the gods
> With verses from the Veda, and they heard him.
> Thus was the boy released from sacrifice
> And Harischandra restored to health.[1]

It would require a strong imagination to fancy that this resembles the story of Isaac—that the character of the avaricious hermit was like that of Abraham!

Surely no one who has read both stories can suppose for a moment that either was borrowed from the other, and possibly it would not be too much to conjecture that those who make these uncritical assertions have never read either of the narratives in question!

[1] Aitareya-brah., Haug's ed., 7–13, Williams's trans.

*The Gita-govinda.* Govinda is the title "Prince of Cows" which was given to Krishna by Indra, and the Gita is the song composed to describe the conduct of Krishna with the wives and daughters of the cowherders, and especially Radha. Some modern writers who were unacquainted with the true character of the Gita, have confidently asserted that "The Song of Solomon was borrowed from the Gita-govinda"!

Here we have another example of the reckless disregard of the principles of scholarly criticism. The author of the Gita-govinda was Jaya-deva, who lived in India in the 12th century of the Christian era, many centuries after the author of the Song of Solomon "slept with his fathers."

# CHAPTER VIII

## IMITATIONS OF THE GOSPELS

Modern Productions. King Herod. The Transfiguration. Crucifixion. Vivekananda.

IT is true there are some similarities to the Gospels in the Puranas, which were written after the Gospels had been in the world for more than a thousand years, but they are so slight that few of them are considered worthy of critical notice.

Attention has been called to a story in the Bhagavata-purana to the effect that Krishna healed a deformed woman who prayed him to allow her to anoint him with saffron and sandal:

> He took compassion upon her and placed his two feet upon her two feet, and his two fingers beneath her chin, and raised her up so that she became quite straight, and by the touch of Krishna, she became young and beautiful.

Thus far, this might possibly be an echo of Mark xiv., and Luke xiii., but the rest of the story is decidedly incongruous, and not at all complimentary to Krishna. Orientalists assign the Bhagavata-purana to the 12th century of the Christian era.

As with the Old Testament, however, so also with the New, we now have speakers and writers who furnish carefully prepared imitations, not of the original texts, which they know nothing about, but of King James's version, giving even the idioms and pecularities of this translation, and then assert that these very modern parodies "were derived from the ancient books of India"!

Books are widely circulated in England and on the Continent, especially in France, as well as in America, which have many paragraphs, and sometimes whole chapters, in imitation of incidents in the life of Christ, and these manufactured quotations are boldly credited to the Bhagavad-gita!

There are several translations of the Gita in our large libraries and some of them have been prepared by Hindu scholars, but a careful examination of even half an hour will convince any one that there is nothing of the kind in the Hindu book from one end to the other. It would have been nearer the truth to say that these things are found in Webster's Dictionary, for the words at least are there, and that is more than we can say for the "Divine Song" of India.

Bhagavad-gita is crudely spelled by this class of writers, each of them apparently guessing at the orthography from a different standpoint, but they usually come near enough to the title so that one can understand what they mean.

Far less fortunate are those pretenders to Oriental lore who talk and write about "The Ramazand, or Hindu New Testament," as no such book is known to scholars, and the pretended quotations from it are simply forgeries of texts which are found only in the New Testament, and sometimes not even there, the copying having been incorrectly done.

If they would take the trouble to *read* the Gospels, it might save them from the blunder of asserting that certain things "were borrowed from the sacred books of India" which are not to be found in either the one or the other!

What can we say, for instance, when it is declared that "The Holy Ghost descended upon *Mary* in the form of a dove"? And that "this statement was taken from the Bhagavad-gita"?

It is confidently declared that: "Jesus of Nazareth borrowed his morals, his doctrines, and even his name from one Jezeus Christna of the Hindus"!

The name of Krishna is thus misspelled apparently for the purpose of confounding his name with that of the Messiah. But the word Christ means "anointed" while Krishna means "black" or "dark coloured." The vast difference in the signification of the names makes it impossible for scholars to suspect any kinship between the two.

And yet, in defiance of all the principles of philology, one author declares: "In Sanskrit, Kristna, or rather Christna, signifies 'messenger of God, promised of God, sacred,' etc." If he had known the meaning of the word Christ he would of course have said that "Christna in Sanskrit means 'anointed'"!

Another of the same class and equally ignorant asserts: "Christna as well as Buddha [enlightened] means shepherd"! Still another of the same reckless sort declares: "Krishna means the sun"!

In relation to Jezeus, one author pretends to quote from the Bhagavad-gita as follows: "They named him Jezeus, that is to say the pure divine essence"! Of course there is nothing of the kind in the Gita, from one end to the other, but on another page of the same book we are assured: "The name of Jesus, or Jezeus, was in ancient India the consecrated epithet assigned to all incarnations"!

The truth is, however, that there is no such name

as Jezeus in Sanskrit—no name like it in the language, and Max Müller declares that "*it was simply invented*" by the author in question.[1]

The above manufactured quotations in relation to "Jezeus" are taken from a French work which has been widely circulated in English translation both in England and America. Poor France is flooded with this spurious literature, the same author having contributed more than twenty volumes to the work of wilfully deceiving the public. He claims that our civilisation, our religion, our legends, and even our God, have come to us from India after passing in succession through Egypt, Persia, Greece, and Italy! "And this statement," he boldly asserts, "has been admitted by almost all Oriental scholars"!

He does not specify any one of them for the best of reasons. He knows, if he knows anything at all about the subject, that no scholar would admit anything of the sort—he knows that such assertions are not made by learned men, but are propagated by people who wilfully deceive the ignorant and unsuspecting victims of their falsehoods!

His allegations that "the Old and New Testaments are found in the Veda," he proves (?) by

[1] Max Müller, *Trans. Vic. Inst.* vol., xxi., p. 179.

such forgeries as his parody on Adam and Eve.[1]

In relation to these colossal falsehoods, Prof. F. Max Müller says: "No one acquainted with Sanskrit or Pali literature can doubt for a single moment that all of these so-called 'translations' from ancient Sanskrit text are mere inventions."[2]

Although Krishna is one of the later products of Indian fancy, having attained his popularity as a god in the Middle Ages of the Christian era, still there are people who know nothing of the subject and are not willing to learn, who are reckless enough to rush into print with the assertion: "Krishna lived 3000 years before Christ, and taught everything that Christ taught"! And still this writer has steadily turned away from sources of information on this subject which are within easy reach in the libraries!

All sorts of pretenders to Indian wisdom are asserting that "Krishna was born of a virgin," and this too in direct violation of the teaching of standard Hindu works on the subject.[3] Surely even a myth ought to be honestly represented! Although the most revolting descriptions of the immorality of this god are given in the native

[1] See p. 144. [2] Max Müller, *Last Essays*, Second Series, p. 95.
[3] See p. 104.

classics, which are devoted to his glorification, we are now assured that "Krishna lived chastely and prescribed chastity," and "Indeed Christianity would have sunk into oblivion ages ago, if the authors of the Gospels had not incorporated into their works the sublime *morale* of Christna"!

When such brazen falsehoods can be uttered and published without fear of contradiction from the masses, surely it is time for the masses to learn some of the facts in the case!

*King Herod.* It is possible that we may have an imitation of the character of King Herod in Kansa, who is represented in the Puranas as a murderous tyrant. It is said:

> After the marriage of Vasu-deva and Devaki . . . a voice from the sky addressed Kansa and said, "The eighth child of the damsel shall take away your life." On hearing this, Kansa drew his sword and was about to put Devaki to death; but Vasu-deva interposed saying: "Kill not Devaki, and I will deliver to you every child she shall bring forth." Appeased by the promise Kansa desisted from the attempt.[1]

Afterward, Kansa was again warned by Narada, but agreeably to his promise Vasu-deva delivered to the tyrant each child as soon as it was born,

[1] Vishnu-purana, p. 493.

to the number of six, these having been the offspring of the demon Hieranyakasipu.[1]

Bala-rama appears to have been the first son of Devaki who was the child of her husband and he was saved by being transferred to the womb of another wife by the name of Rohina. When Krishna, the eighth child of his mother, was born, his father exchanged him with Yasoda for her daughter.

When Kansa was told that a daughter had been born to Devaki he went to the home of Vasu-deva, and seizing the infant, he threw her against a stone; but the child rose into the sky and expanded into a gigantic figure having eight arms, each wielding a powerful weapon. This terrific being laughed aloud and said: "What avails it to thee to have hurled me to the ground? He is born who shall kill thee. . . . Now quickly secure him and provide for thine own welfare."

Kansa, much troubled in mind, summoned his chiefs to counsel:

> Now Chiefs of the Daitya race . . . the goddess has been born who has announced to me that he is again alive who in a former birth was my death. Let therefore active search be made upon the earth, and let every boy in whom there are signs of unusual vigour be slain without remorse.[2]

[1] Vish.-pur., p. 498.

[2] *Ibid.*, 503-4.

The Bhagavata-purana tells the story somewhat differently, but they both describe "Nanda and the rest" as paying tribute or taxes to Kansa. And as the Gospels had been carried to India hundreds of years before these books were written, it is not impossible that we have here a mutilated echo of the narrative found in Matt. ii.

*The Transfiguration.* It is occasionally claimed that the sublime scene on the Mount of Transfiguration "was borrowed from the Bhagavad-gita," which must have been written many years afterward.

There has been considerable discussion concerning the age of the Gita. Prof. Max Müller places it in what he terms the "Renaissance period of Indian literature," the beginning of which he places at about 300 A.D. Sir Monier Monier-Williams says of the author: "He is supposed to have lived in India about the second or third century of our era."[1] We might also quote Weber, Lassen, Lorinser, and others. But in the eagerness to make a point by those who have jumped to the conclusion that the Gospels were borrowed, little anachronisms of one or two centuries are considered entirely unworthy of notice.

[1] Williams, *Hind.*, p. 207.

The stubborn fact of the later origin of the Hindu song is not the only reason why the Gospels could not have borrowed from it; the dissimilarities between the two are so striking that no one could suppose that either was taken from the other.

It is very true, as our best scholars admit, that in making translations from the Sanskrit, the great temptation was to choose only the most beautiful portions of the works before them; not only this, but the constant tendency of a refined and poetic nature is to improve whatever passes through his hands.

Max Müller says:

> Whether I am, myself, one of the guilty ones or not, I cannot help calling attention to the real mischief which has been done, and is still being done, by the enthusiasm of those pioneers who have opened the first avenues through the bewildering forest of the sacred literature of the East. They have raised expectations which cannot be fulfilled, fears also, which, as will readily be seen, are ungrounded.[1]

Oriental poetry is indeed largely indebted to the eloquence of the English translators, who in many cases have given it a beauty far above that which is found in the versions of the native linguists.

[1] Max Müller, *Int. Upanishads*, S. B. E.

But let us not therefore censure our scholars; it is the most natural thing in the world to present the best possible phases of the work which is passing through our hands, and the most beautiful myths of the Orient have gained a new radiance under the poetic touch of modern workers.

In *The Light of Asia* Sir Edwin Arnold was writing poetry, not history, and surely no one could be more astonished than he to learn that many members of a wonder-loving public have imagined his fancies to be facts!

He read into a part of Buddha's story beautiful sentiments of which the primitive Buddhists never heard, and lo! in some minds it was immediately supposed that "this is Buddhism"!

As Sir Edwin has illumined *The Light of Asia* with a borrowed radiance, as Fitzgerald has contributed greatly to the harmonious numbers of the *Rubaiyat*, so also has the Bhagavad-gita received a wonderful beauty in passing through the hands of Sir Monier Monier-Williams, who translates as follows:

Having thus said, the mighty Lord of all
Displayed to Arjuna his form supreme,
Endowed with countless mouths and countless eyes,
With countless faces turned to every quarter,
With countless marvellous appearances—

With ornaments, and wreaths, and robes divine,
With heavenly fragrance and celestial weapons.

It was as if the firmament were filled,
All in an instant with a thousand suns,
Blazing with dazzling lustre; so beheld he
The glories of the universe collected
In the one person of the God of gods.

Arjuna, with every hair on his body bristling with awe, bows his head at this vision, and folding his hands in reverence, gives utterance to a passionate outburst of enthusiastic adoration, which is here abridged:

> I see thee, mighty Lord of all, revealed
> In forms of infinite diversity.
> I see thee like a mass of purest light,
> Flashing thy lustre everywhere around.
>
> I see thee crowned with splendour like the sun
> Pervading earth and air immeasurable,
> Boundless, without beginning, middle, end,
> Preserver of imperishable law,
> The everlasting man; the triple world
> Is awestruck at this vision of thy form
> Stupendous, indescribable in glory.[1]

The late Mr. Justice Kashinath Trimbak Telang, of the Bombay High Court, has given us a *literal* translation of the Gita, and the strength of the

[1] Gita, chap. xi, Williams, *Hind.*, p. 215.

position regarding the poetic work of English scholars cannot be better illustrated than by giving Judge Telang's prose version of the scene which has just been quoted from Williams. The celebrated Hindu linguist translates as follows:

Arjuna stood before him with bowed head, his hair standing on end, and said: "O god I see your body; the gods, as also all the groups of various beings, and the Lord Brahman on his lotus seat, and all the sages and celestial snakes. I see you, who are of countless forms, possessed of many arms, stomachs, mouths, and eyes, on all sides. . . . I see you void of beginning, middle, end, of infinite power, having the sun and moon for eyes; having a mouth like blazing fire, and heating the universe with your radiance. . . . Looking at this wonderful and terrible form of yours, O high-souled one! the three worlds are affrighted, for here these groups of gods are entering into you . . . seeing your mighty form with many mouths and eyes, with many arms and thighs, and feet—with many stomachs, and fearful jaws, all people, and I likewise, are much alarmed. Seeing your mouths, terrible by reason of the jaws and resembling the fire of destruction, I cannot recognise the various directions.

All the bands of kings . . . together with our principal warriors also, are rapidly entering into your mouths, fearful and horrified. . . . And some of their heads are seen to be stuck in the spaces between the teeth. As the rapid currents of the river's waters run toward the sea alone, so do these heroes of the human world enter your mouths, blazing all around.

. . . Swallowing all these people, you are licking them over and over from all sides of your blazing mouths![1]

This is the literal translation by the noted Hindu scholar of the so-called "transfiguration of Krishna"! This is the description which some men dare assert is similar to the scene on the Mount when: "His face did shine as the sun, and his garment was white as the light"!

*The Crucifixion.* Every possible effort has been made to prove that leading events in the life of Christ "were borrowed from the story of Krishna." In furtherance of this scheme it has even been asserted that Krishna was crucified, and this too in the face of the assertion in several of their sacred books to the effect that Krishna was shot by a hunter who mistook him for a wild animal! This statement is made in the Mahabharata and is repeated in their standard works as late as the 11th and 12th centuries of the Christian era.

The author in writing to Sir Monier Monier-Williams not long before his death, alluded among other things to the modern claim that Krishna

[1] Gita, chap. xi., Telang's trans., pp. 93–130.

was crucified, but the eminent *savant* replied: "*I know nothing of this absurd myth!*"

But although it had never until then, reached the higher circles of scholarship, the story was, and is, freely circulated by irresponsible writers and speakers both in England and America as well as on the Continent. Only now and then, however, do we find those who have the temerity to assure their dupes that "Christna was crucified between two thieves, descended into hell, rose from the dead, and ascended into heaven"! And also: "Both Hindu and Christian New Testaments record that at the crucifixion of these two Saviours there was darkness and convulsions of nature"!

We are not only told, in plain contradiction of the Hindu authorities, that "Krishna was crucified," but scholars are actually censured for keeping this important information (?) from the world!

An English author says:

> Neither in the *Transactions* of the Royal Asiatic Society, nor in the works of Sir William Jones is there a single word to be met, concerning the crucifixion of Krishna! How strange that all these writers should be ignorant of so startling a fact!

This last sentence is in italics, and the charge is boldly made, both here and elsewhere, that Orientalists have deliberately and dishonestly withheld this important fact (?) from the people!

We are also assured that Ixion, Prometheus, and Buddha were crucified! The high school pupils know that there is nothing of the kind in the classics concerning either Ixion or Prometheus, and as for Buddha, so far from being crucified, he died in consequence of eating too much pork!

A full account of his illness and subsequent death from this cause is found in the Maha-parinibbana Suttana, or *Book of the Great Decease.*[1] This is considered the oldest and most reliable of the Buddhist works, and being one of the series of "The Sacred Books of the East," it is now available to the English-speaking world.

But what matters it, so far as the Gospel history is concerned, if all these and more had been represented as having suffered thus?

Indeed one author coolly declares: "They were all crucified except Jesus of Nazareth, who was never on a cross"! Not only this, but he claims to prove his baseless assumption by forging quotations (?) from Irenæus, one of the early Christian Fathers, who was born about one hundred and fifty years after Christ. Irenæus, who enunciates the Apostles' Creed in almost the very

[1] Maha-parinibbana Suttana, chap. iv.

words in which it is to-day recited in our churches! Irenæus, who writes of "Our Lord, of his cross and his passion"—of his "having suffered under Pontius Pilate"—Irenæus, whose entire work of two large volumes was written in defence of the doctrines of the Christ—who quotes the old Testament prophecies as pointing to the birth, crucifixion, and resurrection of our Lord![1] An author could not be more grossly misrepresented than in this case.

*Vivekananda.* During the World's Parliament of Religions, held in Chicago in 1893, this Hindu priest stood up in a crowded hall and in violation of all the rules of the Congress, which decreed that no speaker should in any way reflect upon others, he said: "I am told that the American people are so 'liberal' that they will stand criticism." Then he outraged every principle of courtesy and politeness to his hosts, by proceeding to pour out sneers and bitter denunciations upon our missionaries to India. "If they want to help our people," he shouted, "why don't they send them something to save their starving bodies?"

Vivekananda either knew, or he ought to have

[1] See Irenæus, vol. i., pp. 297, 300, 301, 303, 304, 311, 346; also vol. ii., pp. 70, 139, 183, 184, etc.

known, that England and America had sent millions of money and cargoes of grain to "save their starving bodies"!—had sent it in response to appeals from these same Christian missionaries whom he was then slandering! And since that time other millions of money and other cargoes of grain have been sent from the same sources in response to other pleas from the same philanthropic men and women.

During the famine of 1896–7, three years after his insulting assaults upon the best friends India has ever had, not less than fifty millions of dollars were sent from Christian countries for the relief of that hungry and priest-ridden people.

Vivekananda either knew, or he ought to have known, that there were no hospitals in India until they were built under Christian influence, and by Christian money. He either knew, or he ought to have known, that the natives died like flies, near the palaces of the rajas, with no hand to even give them a drink of water, until they were cared for by heroic men and women who followed in the footsteps of Him who "went about doing good." Vivekananda either knew, or he ought to have known, that men, women, and children had been saved from torture and from death by these same loyal souls. He either knew, or he ought to have known, that the women medical missionaries from Christian lands have carried to the women of India timely relief from untold and unnoted agonies.

Dr. John Henry Barrows gladly added his enthusiastic testimony to that of many other travellers concerning the unselfishness and devotion of our missionaries in India, while Theodore Roosevelt and William Howard Taft give enthusiastic praise to the results of their valiant efforts in other lands.

It is not "liberality" which induces our people to applaud these speakers, when they malign and misrepresent the heroes who have gone at America's bidding to heal and relieve the suffering millions of India. It is not "liberality" which induces them to countenance, by their repeated presence, any speaker who attacks the character of the Christ—who induces them to believe stories which are a slander upon his name. Let us not confuse our terms—it is not "liberality," it is *treachery!*

What should we think of a man who would go repeatedly and gladly listen to a speaker who ridiculed or slandered his mother, or other things which are even more sacred? Should we think that he had any right to go around admiring himself, and boasting of his "liberality"? God help the men and women who are willing to give their time, and their money, to those who are doing their utmost to bring shame and reproach and dishonour upon "the only name under heaven, given among men, whereby we must be saved."

# CHAPTER IX

## HINDUISM AND CHRISTIANITY

The Historic Christ. Alleged Life in India. Contrasts. Non-Christian Bibles. The Triumphant Christ.

IT is freely charged that the Messiah is a sun-god—that his personality is fictitious, and has been borrowed from the son-gods of Babylonia, of Egypt, of India or Persia; they are not at all certain *where* it has been borrowed from, but both history and literature have been grossly misrepresented by irresponsible writers on this subject. It requires only a little fair investigation, however, to expose the falsity of their claims.

The historical proofs of the existence of the Christ cannot be given within a small compass; it would require a volume to adequately treat the various lines of evidence on this point, but one thought, at least, may be suggested and this is self-evident.

Whoever stops to think at all, must be aware of the fact that about nineteen hundred years ago some being appeared upon this earth who had influence enough to change the chronology of the whole civilised world, and if it were not Jesus of Nazareth, surely it is time to enquire who it may have been.

The world no longer counts time from A. U. C. (*Anno Urbis Conditæ*), the year in which the City (of Rome) was founded, and only among certain peoples does any one attempt to reckon from the time of the Creation.

The standard time measurement is from B.C.—*Before Christ;* and A.D.—*Anno Domini, in the Year of Our Lord.*

Hence every time an unbeliever dates a letter, or any other document, he testifies to the truth of the first coming of the historic Christ—he bears witness to the fact that it has been nineteen hundred years, and more, since he came and changed the chronology of the nations, besides leaving in a thousand other ways the impress of his undying influence upon the world. This great fact is only one witness in the case, but even this is enough for reliable historical purposes.

*Alleged Life in India.* Even while declaring on the one hand that "no such person as Christ ever existed," the same class of speakers at other times, and before different audiences, are glibly asserting that: "He spent his youth in India, where he learned his Gospel from the priests"! In some instances both these positions are taken by the same author, in the same volume, but little inconsistencies like these being considered unworthy of notice, no effort is made towards a reconciliation.

One man in Chicago published a book to prove that no such being as Jesus of Nazareth ever existed, and afterward delivered a lecture to prove that Jesus was a Socialist! And still his blind followers were entirely unable to see any contradiction between the two positions!

In relation to India, the argument at first ran like this: "No one knows where Christ was during a certain period of his life, therefore he *must* have been in India"!

But, after a time, even its advocates were enabled to understand that this sort of logic was not quite consistent, and in order to save the theory, it became necessary to manufacture "positive proof" on this subject.

Hence it was claimed that certain documents have been "discovered" among Tibetan manuscripts, giving an account of the "Life of Issa in India," and some people talk about "The Unknown Life of Christ" with as much assurance as others will sometimes discourse on "The Secret Will of God"!

It is true that it would not take a clever pandit long to prepare such a manuscript on pages which had been properly "aged," but it has not been necessary for the Hindus to take the trouble to do so. This time the crime lies at the door of a European, and while some other evidence (?) has been manufactured, the most ingenious work of the kind is that of a cunning Russian who produced a bit of fiction which was, and is, very attractive to his dupes. It has passed through eleven editions in poor France, some of whose people are eagerly looking for something of the sort, and it was translated into English before any one found time to make a long and difficult journey, in order to either verify the truth of the story, or to expose a wilful fraud.

To be sure it never deceived scholars, for, as Max Müller said: "One might as well look for the waters of the Jordan in the Brahmaputra, as for a life of Christ in Tibet."

There is much internal evidence which betrays the true character of the book to those who are accustomed to the analysis of evidence, but many have been found who were entirely deceived by this gross imposition, and some of them were very jubilant over it, especially the younger generation of Hindus who were being educated at the expense of the British Government.

This class is well represented by the editor of a Bengali paper, who greeted the "find" as "clear proof that Christianity, like Buddhism, is simply an offshoot from Hinduism, and that Jesus Christ learned his doctrines from the Brahmans"!

It is true there is a space in the history of Christ, and every possible advantage has been taken of this absence of data. The author of this fraudulent work asserts that during that time Christ was in India—that he studied Sanskrit and Pali, that he read the Vedas and the Buddhist canon, and then returned to Palestine to preach the gospel which he had thus learned from these sources.

This writer claims to have gone to the Buddhist monastery at Himnis, where he held long philosophical conversations with the chief Lama, and strange to say, his interpreter on this occasion was a *Shikari!*

> The Kashmeri *Shikari* [says Joldan] is invariably a man whose knowledge of language is limited to his native tongue, and a few words of Urdu and English, relating to the necessities of the road, the camp, and sport, picked up from the English and their attendants.

The Russian claims to have received from the Chief Lama long historical allusions, and complicated philosophical speculations. He quotes the Chief Lama as saying, "The documents brought from India to Nepal, and from Nepal to Tibet, concerning Issa's existence, are written in the Pali language, and are now at Lassa; but a copy in our language, that is Tibetan, exists in this convent."

It was while he was laid up in the convent with a broken leg that he had the opportunity to quote so freely from these documents, which were generously translated to him for this purpose by an ignorant peasant!

Finding that these statements were often accepted by people who do not investigate for themselves, Mr. J. Archibald Douglas, a professor in the Government College at Agra, decided to give the matter a thorough sifting. With this object in view, he went to the Himnis monastery, and found the Superior to be a venerable man who had been so long in office that he must have been the man interviewed by the Russian, if there had been any truth in his story.

But when portions of the book in question were translated to the old chief, he repeatedly exclaimed indignantly: "*Sun, sun, sun, manna dug!*" which is Tibetan for "*Lies, lies, lies, and nothing else!*"

The old gentleman was most courteous, and evidently truthful, but he was justly indignant at the fraud which had been so deliberately perpetrated. Prof. Douglas asked many questions of him, and others in the neighbourhood, and became entirely satisfied that no Russian with a broken leg had ever been there, and no such document as he described had ever been in the convent, or had been heard of there.

A sufficient statement was made out, and it was then sworn to by the Chief Lama in the presence of Archibald Douglas and Mr. Shamwell Joldan, the late postmaster of Ladakh, and the official papers were sent to Prof. F. Max Müller.

Not long before his death the great philologist wrote a magazine article on this subject in which he says:

> After the complete refutation, or I should say the annihilation of N —— by Mr. Douglas, there does not seem to be any excuse for trying to spare the feelings of the venturesome Russian traveller (?). He was not hoaxed, he tried to hoax us.
>
> Mr. Douglas has sent me the original papers, containing the depositions of the Chief Priest of the monastery of Himnis, and of his interpreter, and I gladly testify that they entirely agree with the extracts

given in the article, and are signed and sealed by the Chief Lama, and by Mr. Joldan, formerly postmaster at Ladakh, who acted as interpreter between the priests and Mr. Douglas.

I ought, perhaps, to add that I cannot claim any particular *merit* in having proved the Life of Christ taken from MSS. in the monasteries of Tibet to be a mere fiction.[1]

*Contrasts.* However familiar Christ may have been with the doctrines of Hinduism, it is certain that he never taught them and every system has a right to demand that it be judged by the teaching of its own sacred books.

Even in the morning of its life when it was simple nature worship it was not only different—it was *opposite* in its substance to God's truth, even though all religions may still retain some traces of the primitive revelation made to mankind.

(1) It is the sound, the intonation of the sacred Sanskrit as well as of the sacred Arabic, which is of primary importance and efficacy. Hence millions of people have been obliged to hear, and many of them have been compelled to repeat, the Veda, following the intonations of the teacher, when they had no conception of the meaning of the passages recited.

The books of the Bible, on the other hand, de-

[1] Max Müller, *Nineteenth Century*, vol. xxxix., pp. 667–678.

mand the closest attention of the student, and in order to be of benefit, their meaning must be taken into the hearts, *and lived out in the lives of men!*

(2) Both the Hindus and Arabs were opposed to the translation of their sacred books, the Brahmans especially doing all in their power to prevent publication, even in Sanskrit, while Christian men and women are making great efforts by the expenditure of both time and money to spread the good news of the Gospel. So far from hiding the Book from the fires of investigation, the closest examination is invited everywhere in the world of letters, and not only this but the hosts of criticism are often led by reverent believers.

Great sacrifices have been made, and are being made, to further the colossal work of carrying this great civiliser to the uttermost parts of the earth. Savage dialects have been reduced to grammar for the first time, by enthusiastic missionaries, who have devoted their lives to the task, and so faithfully has the enterprise been pushed that translations have been made, either of the whole, or of some portions of the Book into about five hundred and fifty different languages and dialects, and its circulation is constantly increasing.

The science of philology will always be indebted

to those who have thus led the way in intellectual as well as ethical progress.

(3) In the Veda the historical element is wholly wanting. In all of this mass of literature, there is not a single reliable historical event, which will enable scholars to assign it to its proper place in the world's history, and as we have no Indian manuscripts which extend farther back than the Middle Ages, it is no wonder that Orientalists find it difficult to bridge over this chasm, of possibly two thousand years!

But the races of the Old Testament are prominent figures in history, and not only this, but the statements there made have been illustrated and verified by the spade of the explorer. Ancient cities there described, which were sometimes pronounced "mythical," have been identified, and the very language of the old inscriptions has helped to elucidate difficult passages in the Hebrew Bible.

Says Prof. A. H. Sayce, of Oxford University: "Between the history of the monuments, and the history of the Bible, there is perpetual contact; and the voice of the monuments is found to be in strict harmony with that of the Old Testament." [1]

[1] Sayce, *Assyria, Her Princes and People*, p. 16.

(4) The books of Hinduism reveal no conception of man's nature, while Our Father "remembereth that we are dust."

(5) Hinduism claims that we should crush out all emotion—love as well as hatred, and even indifference (if possible) should be avoided.

But the Master saith: "Thou shalt love the Lord thy God with all thy heart, and with all thy soul, and with all thy mind . . . and thou shalt love thy neighbour as thyself. On these two commandments hang all the law and the prophets."

(6) The gods of Hinduism care nothing for the world—they take no interest in humanity, according to their own exponents.

On the other hand: "Are not five sparrows sold for a farthing, and not one of them is forgotten before God. . . fear not therefore, ye are of more value than many sparrows."

(7) The books of Hinduism admonish men to get rid of the trials and temptations of life. But the Bible says: "Blessed is the man that *endureth temptation*, for when he is tried, he shall receive the crown of life, which the Lord hath promised to them that love him."

(8) Hinduism admonishes us to get rid of all

action, while practical Christianity is the embodiment of wholesome activity:

"My Father worketh hitherto, and I work. . . . By their works, ye shall know them."

(9) Hinduism teaches its devotees to sit for years in one painful posture, until the limbs wither, and the nails grow through the back of the hand. In this attitude they command the admiration of the passers-by.

But under the mission of the Christ the blessing is given to those who: "For my name's sake hast laboured and hast not fainted."

(10) The priests of Hinduism sell to their victims, water from the so-called "Well of Purification"—water reeking with the stench of corruption and laden with the germs of disease.

But the Christ offers "without money and without price" water from the "Wells of Salvation." "Whosoever drinketh of the water that I shall give him shall never thirst, but it shall be in him a well of water springing up to everlasting life."

(11) Hinduism says: "Perform penance, and accumulate merit."

But the Bible says: "By grace are ye saved, and that not of yourselves. It is the gift of God, not of works, lest any man should boast."

(12) Hinduism says: "Get rid of suffering—get rid of feeling."

But the Apostle says: "We glory in tribulation, knowing that tribulation worketh patience, and patience hope."

(13) Hinduism says: "Get rid of the body."

But the Bible says: "Know ye not that your body is the temple of the Holy Spirit which is in you?"

(14) Hinduism teaches men to seek annihilation as the only refuge from repeated rebirths—teaches its devotees to seek *eternal death!*

But the biblical admonition is: "Seek for glory, immortality, *eternal life!*"

(15) The priests of Hinduism spend their time in washing, dressing, painting, and worshipping idols—in bringing oblations, even of food, to gods of wood and stone.

But the servants of the Living God are working night and day for the welfare of the race.

(16) All the history of Hinduism is marked by continual and increasing degradation,—the modern systems containing vileness that could not be entertained by the writers of the early Songs of the Vedas.

But in God's plan, whatever race is willing to follow, is led onward and upward, from the object-lessons in the wilderness, to the triumphant mission of the Christ.

God's book records the sin of the first man, but it advances calmly and surely to the one great end—the conquest of wrong by him who "brought life and immortality to light."

It moves with stately step from Eden lost, to Eden regained, and closes with a splendid panorama of victory.

*The Non-Christian Bibles.* Some traces of God's primeval revelation to man are found among all peoples and in all creeds, but F. Max Müller, in his address before the British and Foreign Bible Society, said:

> Let us teach Hindus, Buddhists, and Mohammedans that there is only one "Sacred Book of the East" that can be their mainstay in that awful hour, when they pass alone into the unseen world. It is that Sacred Book which contains the saying that "*Christ Jesus came into the world to save sinners.*"

He also admonishes students to examine carefully the faith of other nations, for, he says:

> We shall learn to appreciate better than ever before what we have in our own religion. No one who has

not examined patiently, and honestly, the other religions of the world can know what Christianity really is, or can join in such truth and sincerity in the words of St. Paul: "I am not ashamed of the Gospel of Christ."

And again:

Let us see what other nations have had, and still have, in place of religion; let us examine the prayers, the worship, the theology, even of the most highly civilised races—the Greeks, the Romans, the Hindus, the Persians, and we shall then understand more thoroughly what blessings have been vouchsafed to us, in being allowed to breathe, from the first breath of life, the pure air of Christian light and knowledge.

We are too apt to take the greatest blessings as a matter of course, and even religion forms no exception to the rule. We have done so little to gain our religion—we have suffered so little in the cause of truth, that however highly we prize our Christianity, we never prize it highly enough, until we have compared it with the religions of the rest of the world.[1]

Sir Monier Monier-Williams, the Boden Professor of Sanskrit at Oxford University, was the author of eighteen standard works and translations in the domain of Indian wisdom one of them being our great Sanskrit and English Dictionary. After devoting fifty years of his life to this subject, he said:

We welcome these books. We ask every missionary to study their contents . . . but we warn him that

[1] Max Müller, *Chips*, vol. i., pp. 48, 180.

there can be no greater mistake than to force these non-Christian bibles into conformity with some degree of development, and then point to the Christian's Holy Bible as the crowning point of religious evolution!

So far from this, the non-Christian bibles are all *developments in the wrong direction*, they all begin with some flashes of light, and end in utter darkness.

I know that to confess sympathy with this sort of development is to win applause from certain classes in these days of religious toleration and free trade; but I maintain that this flabby, jellyfish kind of tolerance is utterly incompatible with the nerve and backbone that ought to characterise a manly Christian. The Christian's character ought to be just what the Bible intended it should be. Take that sacred Book of ours; handle reverently the whole volume; search it through from the first chapter to the last, and mark well the spirit that pervades the whole.

You will find no limpness, no flabbiness about its utterances. Even sceptics who dispute its authority are ready to admit that it is a thoroughly manly book. Vigour and Manhood breathe on every page. It is downright and straightforward—bold and fearless, rigid and uncompromising. It tells you and me to be either hot or cold. If God be God, serve him; if Baal be God, serve him.

We cannot serve both—we cannot love both. "*Only one name is given among men whereby we may be saved.*" No other Saviour more suited to India, Persia, China, or Arabia is ever mentioned.

The unparalleled declarations of our Holy Bible make a gulf between it and the so-called "Sacred Books of the East" which sever the one from the other, utterly, hopelessly, and for ever. Not a mere rift, across which the Christian and the non-Christian may shake hands, and interchange similar ideas in regard to essential truths, but a veritable gulf which cannot be bridged by any science of religious thought—yes a bridgeless chasm, which no theory of evolution can ever span.

Go forth then, ye missionaries in your Master's name. Go forth into all the world, and after studying all of its false religions and false philosophies—go forth and fearlessly proclaim to suffering humanity the plain, the unchangeable, the eternal facts of the Gospel!

Dare to be downright, with all the uncompromising courage of your own Bible, while with it your watchwords are love, joy, peace, and reconciliation. Be fair, be charitable, be Christlike, *but let there be no mistake*. Let it be made absolutely clear that Christianity cannot, must not, be watered down to suit the palate of either Hindu, Buddhist, or Mohammedan; and that whosoever wishes to pass from any false religion to the true can never do so by the rickety plank of compromise, or by the help of faltering hands, held out by half-hearted Christians. He must leap the gulf in faith, and the living Christ will spread his everlasting arms beneath, and land him safely on the Eternal Rock![1]

*The Triumphant Christ.* "*Let not your hearts be troubled*," God's eternal truths, like His eternal stars, shine on, for ever above and beyond the feeble attacks of man.

[1] Williams, *Trans. Vic. Inst.*, vol. xxi., p. 302.

The world hath many sages, but only one Saviour. The story of the Christ was prefigured in the very morning of time, when the constellations of the cross flashed their glories down upon the new-born earth. What wonder that the children of men learned to love the sacred symbol, even before they understood its meaning?

The centuries come, and the centuries go, but the Cross still bends in southern skies; and in our own heavens the Great Northern Cross is still set with her crown jewels. These are the twofold promise and prophecy of redemption, written in letters of living light, where all the races of the world may read their sublime message.

With nothing to fear, and nothing to hide, Christianity presents as her model, a character who hath no rival in the world's history. Under the leadership of the Great Captain of our Salvation, she shall carry her banners to victory on the glory-crowned heights of God's eternal mountains. Far over and above the worship of the dark idols, there stands the ever-living Son of God. From his stainless life, and cruel cross, the hope of the world was born. One sentence from his lips, if lived out in the lives of men, would for ever banish the pages of wrong and fraud and cruelty from our tear-wet and blood-stained earth. One touch from his hand hath broken the cold seal of the death-angel, and brought immortality to light. One mark of his footstep left in earth's tomb illumines its portals with the glorious promise of *life*. One word from his lips shall lead his risen host to the fountains of living waters, that flow from underneath the Great White Throne.

He is "the bright and the morning star" who shall crown with glory the long dark night of time. He is the Sun of Righteousness with healing in his rays. He shall banish darkness and sorrow and pain—*he shall conquer death*, and illumine with light and life and love the coming ages of God's eternal years.

# BIBLIOGRAPHY


## A

*Aitareya Brahmana.* Sacred Books of the East.
*Asiatic Researches*, vol. v.
AUSTIN, Judge HENRY. *New England Magazine.*

## B

BADSHAH, BHAGWANLAL R. *Transactions Congress of Orientalists.*
BAIJNATH LALA, Ex-Chief Justice. *Transactions Cong. Orientalists.*
BARROWS, Dr. JOHN HENRY, Pres. of Oberlin. *Personal Lectures.*
*Bhagavad-gita.* Williams's trans.
*Bhagavata-purana.* S.B.E.
BHANDARKAR, R. G., Vice-Chancellor Bombay University. *Trans. Cong. Orientalists.*
BHATTACHARYA, JOGENDRA NATH. *Hindu Castes and Sects.*
*Brahmanas.* S.B.E.
*Brahmana-satapatha.* Williams's trans.
*Buddha-karita.* Standard work of Buddhists.

## C

CHILDERS. *Pali Dictionary.*
CUNNINGHAM, Major-General. *Archæological Survey of India.*

## D

DAS, DEVENDRA N. *Nineteenth Century*, vol. xx.
DAVIDS, T. W. RHYS. *Buddhism.*
*Dhama-pada.* Precepts of the Law. S.B.E.
DHARMAPALA, Buddhist priest. *World's Congresses.*
*Deva-duta-sutta.* Early Buddhist work.
DOUGLAS, J. ARCHIBALD, Prof. in Government College. *Nineteenth Century*, vol. xx.

## E

EGGELING, JULIUS. Translation of *Brahmanas.*

F

Fergusson, James. *Tree and Serpent Worship.*

H

*Hari-vansa.* S.B.E.
Hommel, Dr. Fritz, Prof. of Semitic Languages at the University of Munich. *Ancient Hebrew Tradition.*

I

Irenæus, Bishop of Lyons (France) latter quarter of 2d Cent. *Writings.*

J

*Jataka Book.* Birth stories of Buddha.
Jones, Sir William. Translations.

L

*Lalita-vistara.* Eighth in series of nine Dhammas.

M

*Maha-bharata.* Brahmanised epic poem.
*Maha-parinibbana Suttana.* Book of the Great Decease. S.B.E.
*Maha-vagga.* Old Pali work.
*Manu, Code of.* Standard of Hindu law.
Mitra, Rajendra Lala. Translation of *Lalita-vistara.*
" " " *Orissa.*
Müller, Prof. F. Max. *Chips.*
" " " " *Last Essays.*
" " " " *Nineteenth Century*, vol. xxxix.

O

Oldenberg, Dr. Herman. Translation text of Pali canon.

P

*Padma-purana.* S.B.E.
Petrie, W. M. Flinders. *Religion of Egypt.*

R

Ramabai Pandita. *High Caste Hindu Woman.*
*Ramayana.* Hindu epic, Griffith's trans.

REED, E. A. *Hindu Literature.*
" " *Primitive Buddhism.*
*Rig-veda.* S.B.E.

S

SAUSSE, Sir MATTHEW, Supreme Court of Bombay. *History of Bombay Maharajas.*
SAYCE, Prof. A. H. *Assyria, Her Princes and People.*
*Sukhavati-vyhua.* Early Buddhist work.

T

TELANG, KASHINATH TRIMBAK, Judge of High Court of Bombay. Translation of *Bhagavad-gita.*

U

*Upanishads.* S.B.E.

V

*Vishnu-purana.* Wilson's translation.

W

WALHOUSE. *Indian Antiquities.*
WHEELER, J. TALBOYS. Translation of *Maha-bharata.*
WILLIAMS, Sir MONIER MONIER-. *Hinduism.*
" " " " *Indian Wisdom.*
" " " " *Brahmanism and Hinduism.*
" " " " *Trans. Vic. Institute.*
WILSON, Prof. HORACE HAYMAN. Translation of Puranas.

# INDEX